WITH MY OWN

The Memoirs of Raymond Lister

Descended from craftsmen on one side and from farmers on the other, Cambridge-born Raymond Lister spent his apprentice years in the family firm before a lifelong involvement with a variety of arts and crafts, from ballet and art history to architectural metalwork, print-making and book production. His memoirs paint a vivid picture of Cambridge after World War I; he also brings into focus such friends as Siegfried Sassoon and Edmund Blunden, Philip Gosse, C.B. Fry, Clifford Bax, Sir Geoffrey Keynes, Kurt Jooss and Rudolf von Laban.

Dr Lister's forthright views extend to religion, ideals in the practice of art and life, and personal problems.

He is a leading authority on Blake and his followers, including Samuel Palmer, Edward Calvert and George Richmond. A chapter on connoisseurship discusses the forgeries of Palmer's work by Tom Keating which he helped to expose; he also appeared as an expert witness at Keating's trial. He has been President of the Royal Society of Miniature Painters, Sculptors and Gravers; Managing Director of the Golden Head Press; President of the Private Libraries Association; Chairman of the Governors of the Federation of British Artists; President of the Architectural Metalwork Association; a Syndic of the Fitzwilliam Museum, Cambridge; Prime Warden of the Worshipful Company of Blacksmiths in the City of London. He is at present an Emeritus Fellow of Wolfson College, Cambridge.

WITH
MY OWN
WINGS

The Memoirs of
Raymond Lister

The Oleander Press

The Oleander Press
17 Stansgate Avenue
Cambridge CB2 2QZ
England

The Oleander Press
80 Eighth Avenue, Suite 303
New York
N.Y. 1011
U.S.A.

© 1994   Raymond Lister and
The Oleander Press

British Library Cataloguing in Publication Data

Lister, Raymond
    With my own wings: memoirs
    I. Title
    700.92

    ISBN 0-906672-66-X

Printed and bound in Great Britain

Contents

List of Illustrations   vii

1. The Listers ...   1

2. The Arnolds ...   11

3. A Cambridge Childhood ...   21

4. My Three Schools ...   36

5. Prentice Years ...   64

6. The Arts Beckon ...   75

7. Ballet and Other Matters ...   83

8. Re-Embarkation ...   102

9. Marriage ...   108

10. Philip Gosse and Friends ...   113

11. Publishing and Book Making ...   123

12. De Profundis ...   138

13. The Followers of William Blake ...   145

14. Dolce Vita ...   153

Biographical Notes ...   161

Books and Pamphlets by Raymond Lister ... 164

Index ...   170

List of Illustrations

Page 1   *Upper:* Myself aged about 6 months, with my mother
          and father on the beach at Great Yarmouth, 1919.
          Lower: John and Annie Elizabeth Arnold, my maternal
          grandparents, with their family, about 1909.
          Standing: My mother, Uncle Jack.
          At Front: Uncle Tom, Auntie Connie, Auntie Ruby,
          Auntie Hilda.

Page 2   *Upper:* Frances Emily Lister, my grandmother.
          Lower: George Lister, my grandfather. Both about 1905.

Page 3   *Upper:* Myself aged about 4 years.
          Lower: Uncle Humphrey Lant, 1929.

Page 4   *Upper:* Ernie Fox operating a centre-lathe, about 1960.
          Lower: Wrought iron panel from Castle Howard,
          Yorkshire conserved in the workshops of George Lister
          and Sons Ltd., about 1955.

Page 5   Silhouette portrait by myself of Albert Cousins, 1952.

Page 6   *Upper:* Design for setting by myself for *Noye's Fludde*,
          produced at the Festival Theatre, Cambridge, 1936.
          Lower: Myself (standing in overalls, centre left) as
          'Numero Quinze' in *Libel!* by Edward Wooll. The
          Festival Repertory Company, 1939. Festival Theatre,
          Cambridge.

Page 7   Myself, 1939.

Page 8   Irina Baronova, 1938.

Page 9   Mary Honer and Leslie Edwards in *Coppélia*, Act II,
          1940.
          Photo: Gordon Anthony. From the collections of the
          Theatre Museum. By courtesy of the Board of Trustees
          of the Victoria and Albert Museum.

Page 10   Kurt Jooss, about 1938.
           Photo. Gordon Anthony. From the collections of the
           Theatre Museum. By courtesy of the Board of Trustees
           of the Victoria and Albert Museum.

Page 11   Sigurd Leeder, about 1935.
           Photo. Gordon Anthony. From the collections of the
           Theatre Museum. By courtesy of the Board of Trustees
           of the Victoria and Albert Museum.

Page 12   *Upper: Snowflake Play.* Children's Game for four groups
           by Jenny Gertz. Opening movements recorded in
           Kine-tography Laban, about 1936.
           Lower: Two pupils of Jenny Gertz in the open-air
           theatre at Dartington Hall, Devon, about 1939.

Page 13   *Left:* Cover of programme of dance recital, arranged by
           myself, 1941.
           Right: Selma Burger, about 1937.

Page 14   Pamela and myself, just married, 1947.

Page 15   Three miniature paintings by myself:
           Upper left: Fionnuala flying over Moyle, 1945. Private
           Collection.
           Upper right: The Unicorn of the Marshes, 1947. Brotherton
           Collection, University of Leeds.
           Lower: The Three Swans, 1956. Private Collection.

Page 16   Two wood-engravings by myself:
           Upper: Church and Crescent Moon, 1956.
           Lower: Yggdrasil, 1958.

Page 17   Two miniature paintings by myself:
           Upper: Hindu Dancer, 1952. Diploma Collection, Royal
           Society of Miniature Painters, Sculptors and Gravers.
           Lower: Hortus Conclusus, 1978. Collection of the late
           Arnold Fawcus, Paris.

Page 18   Myself with Pamela and Rory (aged about 12 months)
           and Arthur Astbury, 1953.

Page 19   Philip Gosse, 1957.

Page 20   Siegfried Sassoon with friend, May 1952.

Page 21   *Upper*: My father, about 1968.
           Lower: My mother, about 1968.

Page 22   Myself with Simon Lissim, about 1960.

Page 23   Rory and Delia entertaining us, Christmas 1964.

Page 24   A group of books, most published by the Golden Head
           Press, designed by myself.

Page 25   The Golden Head Press and other ephemera.

Page 26   Rudolf von Laban, about 1934.

Page 27   *Upper: The Chamber Idyll* by Edward Calvert.
           Wood-engraving, 1831.
           Lower: Harvest under a Crescent Moon by Samuel Palmer.
           Wood-engraving, *circa* 1826.

Page 28   *Upper: The Sleeping Shepherd* by Samuel Palmer,
           Etching, 1857.
           Lower: Illustration by William Blake, for Virgil's First
           Eclogue, from Robert John Thornton's *Pastorals of
           Virgil*. Wood-engraving, 1821.

Page 29   Myself selecting (from photographs) works by Samuel
           Palmer for *Samuel Palmer and 'The Ancients'*, a major
           exhibition held at the Fitzwilliam Museum,
           Cambridge, 1984. Courtesy of *Cambridge Evening News*.

Page 30   Myself with Sir Geoffrey Keynes (Samuel Palmer
           looking on in the background), at the opening of the
           exhibition *Samuel Palmer: A Vision Recaptured*, Victoria
           and Albert Museum, 1978.

Page 31 *Upper:* Myself and Pamela at Linton, on the day I had received my Litt.D., 1990.
Lower: Myself with Irina Baronova in our Cambridge garden, 1992.

Page 32 Pamela, about 1986.

One
The Listers

I was born in my maternal grandfather's now demolished home, Soham House, 113 Newmarket Road, in Cambridge, at 1 o'clock in the morning of an inclement day, 28 March 1919, just over four months after the 1918 Armistice. It was a difficult birth; my mother's ordeal was harrowing, largely, my father claimed, because of a combination of incompetence and callousness on the part of the doctor. Some of her difficulties, however, were probably attributable to the fact that late in her pregnancy, my mother (and my father) had been stricken with, and almost died from, the 'Spanish' influenza which raged through Europe after the end of the Great War.

My father, Horace Lister, an engineer, had served throughout the War, making torpedoes for the Royal Navy. (By coincidence I too worked on Admiralty contracts during World War II.) Most of my ancestors were craftsmen. As far back as Ambrose Lister of Bury St. Edmunds, and Josiah Lister of Great Bradley, Suffolk, both of whom flourished in the second half of the seventeenth century, members of my family have shaped metal and timber and sewn cloth.

My great-grandfather, George, born at Shudy Camps in Cambridgeshire in 1828, was the fourth child and second son of William Lister, an agricultural labourer (an occupation in itself requiring considerable skill). George, a sawyer, practised his hard, laborious craft in an effluvium of sweat, resin and sawdust, vividly described in George Sturt's classic *The Wheelwright's Shop*

1

```
                    AMBROSE LISTER = Ann Starling
                      fl. 1634, Bury St. Edmunds
                                  |
        JOHN 1683-?...............Josiah = Mary
        Bury St. Edmunds    .        fl. 1694, Little Bradley
                            .
                   THOMAS = Sarah Smith
                 fl.1714, Great Bradley, Suffolk
                            |
        THOMAS = (1) Elizabeth Bye; (2) Frances Sanderson
                   1724-65, Great Bradley
                            |
                 SHADRACH = Ann Mansfield
            1762-1834, Shudy Camps, Cambridgeshire
                            |
                 WILLIAM = Harriet Barker
        1799-circa 1851, Castle Camps, Cambridgeshire
                            |
                 GEORGE = Sarah Doncaster
        1827-1903, Castle Camps, March and Cambridge*
                            |
```

| Emma b.1855 | Frederick b.1857 | GEORGE 1858-1930 = Frances Emily Pratt 1856-1945 (my grandparents) | Jane 1860-1926 | Arthur b.1863 | Harry b.1865 | Fanny 1867-1945 |

2

Emily Maude   Alice ('Bet')   Alfred Christopher   HORACE
1884-1960   1886-1976   1888-1928   = Ellen Maud Mary Arnold
= William Smith   = Hubert Gardner   = Maud Kate Lines   (my parents; for my mother's
                                                                 dates, see p.4)

                                    RAYMOND GEORGE b. 1919   Brian Horace b.1926
                                    = Pamela Helen Brutnell   = Joyce Josephine Prest
                                      b. 1925

Rory Brian George b.1952   Delia Fionnuala b.1958
= Sylvia Johnson   = Patrick Campbell

        Alexander George b.1989   Carlo Patrick b.1992   Fionnuala Sarah b. 1994

*From this point the family has lived in Cambridge or nearby.

CHARLES ARNOLD 1842-1912 = (1) Cecilia Mary Nugent 1844?-79?
                          (2) Ellen Gathercole 1842-?

Emmigrated to Bendigo, Victoria, Australia circa 1861; returned
to England and settled in Cambridge 1870

Michael Nugent	Charles	JOHN	Henry	Thomas David	Patrick	William
1863-1927	1865(?)-1933	1867-1933	1869-1951	1871-1953	1873-1913	1876-1932
= Florence Jane	= Ellen(?)	= Annie Elizabeth	= Anne	= Mary Ann	= Alice	= Charlotte
Worboys		Townsend 1864-1941	Thompson	Holmes	Brown(?)	Ann Graveling
		(my grandparents)				

George 1903-55

				Cornelius	Dora Mary	Robert
				William	Rose	Charles
				1902-75	b.1905	b. 1907

| | | | Elsie | David Thomas |
| | | | 1902-79 | 1904-44 |

Cecilia Emma 1897-1974   Ellen Mary ('Max') 1899-1980

Florence Agnes ('Dod') 1908-82

ELLEN MAUD MARY	John Christopher	Hilda 1900-1958	Thomas Frank	Constance	Ruby Marie
1894-1968	(Jack) 1898-1989	= Humphrey Lant	1903-81	Margaret	1908-55 =
(my mother;	= (1) Eileen Horne			1904-81	Thomas Howard
see Horace	(2) Nancy Nicholls				
Lister p.3)					

Note: For their help in compiling the Arnold genealogy, I am grateful to my cousins the late Patrick Arnold, Betty Bendall, Bridget Johnson and Richard Johnson.

4

(1923). I never knew him, for he died in 1903, sixteen years before my appearance. But I do possess his copy of E. Hoppus's *Practical Measurer* of 1826, with pencilled calculations on its endpapers for sawing ash trunks into feather boards, and poplar and oak into planks. I have, too, a William IV penny of 1831, which carries the marks made by his saw as it sliced through the tree trunk in which the coin was embedded. And I have a snapshot, taken in his old age, of him wearing a bowler hat at a somewhat rakish angle and a greatcoat with a moleskin collar, his eyes humorously twinkling.

Several of George Lister's offspring were craftsmen. In particular my grandfather, another George, who was a superlative engineer. Great-Uncle Fred (in appearance almost a clone of my grandfather) was a master fitter, and had a little workshop on Quayside in Cambridge across the river from Magdalene College. Great-Uncles Arthur and Harry were robemakers and tailors. Great-Aunt Fan, their sister, who lived with my grandparents, and was a valued companion of my childhood, was a tailoress, who made among other things fancy waistcoats for Lord Hawke, the celebrated Yorkshire cricketer.

My father and his brother Alfred, both engineers, followed in the family tradition. I use the word engineer advisedly; it usually, I know, connotes professionalism rather than craftsmanship. But no other word could describe a craftsman who, like my grandfather, could operate many different kinds of machine tool, who could install a boiler, a printing machine or for that matter a complete factory, and who could, and did, design and make steam engines. Similarly, my father was not only a skilled mechanic, but was able to design an elaborate wireless receiving set during the fortunate days when those noisy contraptions were both quieter and fewer.

The Listers were not only craftsmen, but also dedicated Nonconformists. My grandfather was a Sunday School teacher and a deacon of St. Andrew's Street Baptist Chapel, where he often preached. He had an enviable simplicity of faith, centred on what was to him the rock-like foundation of the Holy Bible, to which he turned throughout his life for instruction and recreation, and which he held in his hands even on his deathbed. His life was dominated by it; his standards of craftsmanship were

5

conditioned by it. He would no more think of lowering his standards of work than his standards of life, and in time his craftsmanship became an aspect of his religion; it was a way of life as real to him as the Tao to a Taoist.

Not unexpectedly, he ensured, when I was a child, that I was not kept in ignorance of the Scriptures. Often he would take down his big Family Bible, and relate the stories of its illustrations (some of which were taken from the grandiose and apocalyptic visions of John Martin), making them as vivid and exciting as any tale of adventure. I have a little book of Bible stories which has been handed down in the family over many years: *Bible Pictures for Little People* by 'Uncle Harry', whose true identity I have never been able to discover; certain it is that he was not *my* Great-Uncle Harry. Grandad Lister used this book, too, to awaken my interest. Some of the illustrations were horrific, especially that depicting Shadrach, Meshach and Abednego in the burning fiery furnace, sitting nonchalantly amid the flames despite that 'the fire had been made hotter than usual'. The horrific part of this illustration is, however, the destruction of two furnace attendants who are running away in terrified panic as they are consumed by flames. My favourite character in the book was Absalom, the pleasure-seeking son of David, who seemed to me to derive more enjoyment from life than the average Canaanite. His end seemed to me grossly unfair, caught and suspended by his luxuriant locks from the branch of a tree as his horse galloped through the wood of Ephraim.

When I was at school, every Wednesday half-holiday, and until my grandfather died in 1930, I visited my grandparents and Aunt Fan at their (now demolished) house, 6 Cam Road, for luncheon, at which my favourite dishes were invariably served: a first course of boiled batter pudding ('light pudding') and gravy, followed by roast chicken, and rounded off with pink blancmange. The others finished off with cheese, and when Stilton was in season, a whole cheese was always on the table; Grandad used to put a little of its dust in his pocket microscope to show me the tiny spiders in it.

We always lunched in the parlour, in the old-fashioned way; a proper dining room at the front of the house was reserved for important occasions and afternoon tea. After lunch Grandad and I, whom he called 'The Masterpiece' on account of my insatiable curiosity, spent the afternoon talking together or playing games, usually draughts and dominoes, though sometimes I had huge jigsaw puzzles to solve. Granny and Aunt Fan joined us for tea, consisting of home-made lemon curd and strawberry jam, anchovies, sardines, fish paste, potted meat, bread and butter, boiled eggs, strawberry jelly (especially for me), seed cake, fruit cake and sugar-coated biscuits.

Later, when Grandad's weak heart began to affect him, he took a siesta in the afternoon while I played make-pretend games with Aunt Fan, a genius at amusing children, whom she understood perfectly. It was a tragedy that she did not marry and have a family of her own. 'Doctors and nurses' was a favourite game when I was very young. Fan would put a table napkin over her head as a nurse, and I, as doctor, wore an old pair of Grandad's *pince-nez* spectacles. Grandad, our patient, lay on the settee to be examined. 'Doctors and nurses' came to a sudden end one afternoon when I announced that I was going to circumcise the patient!

As for dressing up, that infallible and imaginative way to win the heart of a child, Fan adapted old pyjama suits, discarded dresses and hats for charades. In another great game she made herself a set of false teeth from orange peel, which she put under her lips and then allowed me, with sadistic relish and almost ungovernable excitement, to extract them one by one with Grandad's pliers. Sometimes we hung a linen sheet across the drawing-room bay-window as a screen and, with a light placed behind us, and with the remainder of the room in darkness, Aunt Fan and I gave a shadow-show performance for Granny and Grandad.

Aunt Fan, a virtuosic needlewoman, could transform the most ordinary pieces of spare material into the most delightful garnishings to my activities: a frill for my old dog Mick so that he could be metamorphosed into Dog Toby for my Punch and Judy show, a string of cloth sausages filled with an old stocking for Punch and Joey the clown to cook in their frying pan; and she could make even marionettes. When I stayed with my grandparents, she would race me around the garden so as to give effect to the brimstone and treacle Granny Lister had insisted on my taking to disencumber my bowels.

I recall the home of my Lister grandparents as a living museum of Victoriana. Something I shall always associate with Granny is the redolence of centifolia and moss roses, which she placed in specimen vases, on mats of sad green velveteen, widely edged with lace, and standing on polished mahogany: the whole house during midsummer was permeated with their scent. Each downstairs room had a cast iron and tiled fireplace, with an elaborate chimneypiece above. Some of the pictures I forget, but I recall one in the dining room – a black and white print of a beautiful young lady dressed in white, with her elegant tapered fingers lightly touching the keys of a piano. Her eyes had a distant expression, and a sheepdog sat beside her with his head resting on her lap, regarding her soulfully. The music on the piano was Cardinal Newman's hymn *Lead, Kindly Light*. In the same room were two quite competently executed landscapes in oils by my father's sister, Auntie Bet (Alice), an amateur painter. The sideboard supported a fully charged tantalus, a cut-glass biscuit barrel and, under glass domes, a pair of Parian ware statuettes of female figures representing War and Peace. Placed beside Peace, inside her dome, sat a couple of silver leaves from my grandparents' silver-wedding cake.

The drawing room looked out on to Granny's pretty garden with its box-edged flower beds and gravel paths. Here were two more large prints, of gulls circling in a storm above cliffs battered by gigantic waves, and a chiffonier with the Family Bible, a photograph album bound in black leather containing a photograph which never ceased to impress me: it was taken by firelight and was printed on vermilion paper. There were also a little silver clock, a vase containing a pot of maidenhair fern, and a pair of cowrie shells which Granny made me hold up to my ear so that I could 'listen to the sea'. A picture hung above the chiffonier: a large photograph in an oval frame of my father flanked by his sisters Maude and Bet. In another photograph, Aunt Bet gazed rapturously at a rose. Photographs of Grandad and Granny stood on the chimneypiece in silver frames. Opposite the chiffonier hung an oval mirror of elaborate gilded gesso inset with green velvet, and arms to support ornaments. The wireless set, an incongruous modern element, was housed in a large polished mahogany cabinet standing in an alcove. The furniture was covered in velveteen of a wonderfully resplendent shade of crimson, a colour in itself essentially Victorian.

Most of the dining-room furniture I have forgotten, except two little oval bevelled mirrors mounted with deers' heads of painted whitemetal, with detachable antlers that could be removed after the rutting season: they were among Aunt Fan's few possessions. On the chimneypiece an ugly clock in an oak case bore a brass plaque stating that it was presented to my grandfather on his retirement from his directorship of the Cambridge Foresters' Benefit Building Society, which years before he had helped to establish.

In the parlour, above the fireplace hung a framed lithographed text which read GOD BLESS OUR HOME. It was ghastly, closely related to those plaster tributes so often in evidence years ago under glass domes on graves. Beneath it, on the shelf, stood a busily ticking American clock, in a case shaped like a Gothic arch, with a panel of flowered yellow glass in its door, behind which the pendulum might be dimly discerned. A deal dresser, 'grained' by a decorator, supported a comfortable array of Victorian plates, some with waved fluted rims, others with ivy-leaf patterns, and a little Japanese model chest of drawers, the contents of which always included a nutmeg or two. The cupboards which formed the lower section of the dresser were pungent with herbs and spices.

The parlour also had a hanging bookcase, containing religious books, Mrs Beeton's *Household Management*, Whitaker's *Almanack*, an odd volume of an old encyclopedia, and quantities of Edgar Wallace's novels; and a scrubbed pine table, with a drawer full of hammers, screwdrivers, pliers, knives, string and candles. After lunch a chenille cloth was draped over it, and the parlour shed its workaday appearance.

Little of the contents of the upstairs rooms comes to mind, except for my great-grandparents' photographs, and an early daguerreotype of my great-great-grandfather, William Lister, who was born in 1799. Over my grandfather's bed hung a coloured photograph of Uncle Alf in uniform in France during the Kaiser's War. I also remember a small safe by the wardrobe and Granny's little leather-covered Victorian jewel box, which had a diced pattern all over it, like the one on the cover of the photograph album on the chiffonier downstairs.

Such was the quiet and comfortable home of my grandfather and grandmother as I remember it, which was their pride and joy. It provided the background to many of the happiest and most inspired hours of my childhood.

Two
The Arnolds

*

It may seem surprising that my father, with his strongly Nonconformist background, should have married a Roman Catholic, but love overcomes much and my parents remained very much in love with one another throughout their lives. My mother, Ellen Maud Mary Arnold, was the daughter of John Arnold, a prosperous farmer.

The Arnolds' affluence had been founded by Charles Arnold (John's father), who in 1861 left Gamlingay in Cambridgeshire at the age of nineteen to prospect for gold at Bendigo in Victoria, whence he returned a few years later with his fortune secured, accompanied by his young bride Cecilia (*née* Nugent) an emigrant from Ballynahinch, Co. Tipperary, who was seventeen when he married her. There is a street in Bendigo named after him.

Charles was noted for his open purse. Although he was a Catholic, for his second wife, Ellen, a Nonconformist (Cecilia died young, in childbirth), he characteristically, underwrote the building of the chapel of the Gospel Mission which, until quite recently, stood on Newmarket Road. So widespread was his benevolence, that as his funeral cortège passed through the streets, the pavements were lined with silent and bareheaded poor folk who wished to pay tribute to him. His reputation reached also to other strata of Cambridge society, and among those who attended his funeral was the Master of Trinity College (Henry Montagu Butler), at that time an almost unheard-of mark of respect by a leading member of the University to a local man of trade.

John Arnold, my grandfather, and his brothers were completely different from the Listers, with a measure of Irish extravagance in their make-up. When young, if any trouble was brewing, they were certain to be part of it, if not its instigators. Their father, some time after returning from Bendigo, had set six of them up in partnerships in several farms around Cambridge, and in a flourishing dairy in the town. Each farm had its own resident manager, but the brothers ran the dairy themselves, each working a milk-delivery round; they virtually controlled the local dairy business.

A sense of levity permeated everything they did; even deathbed scenes could be hilarious. When Great-Uncle Pat lay dying, the priest arrived to administer extreme unction, and asked, 'Are you prepared to meet your Creator, my son?' Quickly, though faintly, came Pat's answer; 'Sure. It's the other fellow I'm not prepared to meet!' Many years after this, for Uncle Pat died young, his brother Tom was near death, and his doctor, working hard to bring him relief, asked, 'Are you short of breath, Mr. Arnold?' 'No', said Uncle Tom, 'Short of money!' And Great-Uncle Charlie, desperately ill from gangrene in 1932, had one of his legs amputated during May, the other in the following December. As he was wheeled into the operating theatre for the second time, he sang the old song to the nurses, *Will you treat me in December as you did in May?*

At other times their methods would have done credit to a brigand or a pirate. At the circus, or even at concert parties on the pier during seaside holidays at Great Yarmouth, they invariably paid for the cheapest seats, but sat themselves in the most expensive ones. There were always several of them, big powerful men, and the management was careful not to upset them too much, although in the event any such confrontations resulted in banter rather than fisticuffs. My mother remembered the routine, when she was taken with other children in the family to a circus by her father and three or four of his brothers. A clown came over to the party and pointed out that they were in the wrong seats, only to be met with derisive cries of, 'Quite well, thank you; how are you?'

The Arnolds were, without exception, staunch Conservatives and always worked hard during elections to secure the return of the Tory candidate. Especially enthusiastic, Great-Uncle Tom canvassed indefatigably. During a county council election, the Tory candidate was Major Thomas Musgrave Francis of Quy, a member of an old county family and a noted landowner. Having knocked on the door of a house, Uncle Tom was answered by a lady who looked at him enquiringly. 'I've called to ask if you will vote for Major Francis', said Tom. "I don't see why I should', replied the lady. 'Why not?' said Tom. 'He's as good as the other bugger, isn't he?'

Devotion to the Tories remained – still remains – in the family. When I was a child my mother's cousin Max (a daughter of Great-Uncle Tom) would say, if she saw a scarlet hat or dress, 'Ugh! I hate that, it's Labour!' This must have impressed me. When I was about four years old I was taken by my mother to a Conservative fête at Croxton Park, the seat of our local M.P., Sir Douglas Newton (later Lord Eltisley). Lady Newton came over to speak to Mother, and tried to present me with a scarlet balloon. But I refused to take it. 'What's wrong with it, dear?' asked Lady Newton. 'It's Labour', I said. Her delight was boundless, and she quickly found me another one in pink and white, the local Tory colours.

Why Cambridge did not use the traditional Tory blue I do not know. But pink and white it had always been, until superseded by the ubiquitous blue after World War II. The Tory children in our district had a jingle which they chanted at Liberal children (whose colours were blue and buff):

Pink and white is my delight.
Blue and buff? I hate the stuff.

Many a fight was precipitated by that couplet, but what of Labour's red? That was quite outside the pale, not quite nice to mention, so there was no dismissive jingle for the indication of incipient bloody revolution and regicide suggested by Labour's scarlet.

Of my Arnold grandparents, my grandfather John Arnold was one of the kindest and most open-hearted men I have ever known. I sometimes spent a day with him on his peregrinations in his governess cart around his farms. During these trips he would pull up his pony to speak to any tramp he came across, and never bade him farewell without giving him money, or on at least one occasion, his own packed lunch. When I saw that, I protested, 'Grandad, you'll have nothing to eat!' 'Oh', he said, 'I shall have plenty this evening. Perhaps that poor devil will get nothing.' Quite often working-men with families and down on their luck would call at his house and say they had nothing for their children's meals, and he would immediately take them across the road to the butcher's shop and buy them a joint.

His wife, Granny Arnold, was a most placid woman, whose chief relaxation was to sit in the twilight in the bay window at the front of her house and watch the world go by. She could see a whole parade of it, as Soham House stood on the main road from Cambridge to Newmarket, and she watched a constant flow of traffic and pedestrians, in particular during Newmarket race meetings, at the time of the Mays (rowing races) and during Midsummer Fair on the nearby common. Granny Arnold must have known by sight every regular passer-by.

One of Granny's greatest pleasures was to entertain her cronies to dining-room tea as was then customary (one recalls Rupert Brooke's poem *Dining Room Tea*). On such occasions the dining table was covered with a dazzlingly white and somewhat stiff, lace-edged linen cloth on which was arranged a feast consisting of rich fruit- and sponge-cakes of her own creation, standing on cut-glass cake-stands with linen and lace doyleys; plates of delicious home-baked crusty bread and butter fresh from the dairy; home-made jams; vases of celery and lettuce; dishes of sardines and anchovies; and, in season, a cut of freshly-boiled salmon. This gargantuan repast would be served on the best china, and Grandma presided at the head of the table with a large silver pot of fragrant tea before her. The ladies maintained a constant flow of chatter, nearly all of it centred on small talk and occasionally minor scandals, revolving around their own social circle.

Like many placid people, Granny Arnold had a decidedly insensitive streak in her character. This is vividly illustrated by her treatment of my mother when she was a little girl of four years;

she had hung up her stocking on Christmas Eve, but when she awoke in the morning and rushed excitedly to the foot of the bed, she discovered her stocking as empty as it had been when she hung it up. Bursting into tears she ran to her mother who blandly informed her that Father Christmas had fallen down and spilled all his toys. When my grandfather heard about this, he immediately took my mother out, and loaded her with toys; but the magic had departed. Yet Granny never turned a beggar away, rarely uttered an unkind word to anybody, and could not have been more amiable to me. Human character can be full of such unexpected contradictions.

****

Across the road, exactly opposite Granny Arnold's bay window, lived Great-Uncle Tom and his wife, Aunt Mary Ann. Uncle Tom lived in a perpetual hurry; he spoke in a hurry, with hardly a pause between words, he worked in a hurry, he walked in a hurry; I am sure he even slept in a hurry. His bustle sometimes led him into difficulties: one day he walked into the hall, took a quick step towards the staircase, and fell over on to his back on the highly polished linoleum. Aunt Mary Ann, muttering imprecations against the maid (who had only done her job too enthusiastically), took a bucket of sand from the garden, and threw the contents over the polished surface. "I'll not have my Tom falling over like that', she declared.

Aunt Mary Ann's ancient mother lived with the family. Much admired by Uncle Tom, who often claimed he would not part with her for ten thousand pounds, Granny Holmes was a little grim and grey old lady with a set, disgruntled visage who dressed in black in the fashion of the 1860s. Pinned on her dress was a brooch made from a crown piece: the only item of decoration she allowed herself. In her command of oaths and expletives she excelled, as her rent-collector found one day to his embarrassment. Granny owned several houses in the district, the drains of one of which had for a considerable period given rise to problems. The rent-collector delivered his takings to her one Monday with the news that the drains were blocked once again. 'What!' shrilled Granny, 'do the buggers shit bullets?' The wretched collector, a deacon at the local Nonconformist tabernacle was reduced to whispering, 'Oh hush, Mrs Holmes, hush!'

Tom and Mary Ann's domestic staff included at least two noteworthy eccentrics. George Careless, their elderly groom, was a goblin-like little man with faded ginger hair and moustache, who seemed permeated always by the pleasant aroma of the stable. When I was little he invariably greeted me with, "Ullo! When's yer grandad going to buy yer a darnkey?' I should have loved one, but he never did. My grandfather did buy me an attractive dapple-grey rocking horse, whose tail and mane he dressed with coloured ribbons like a show horse's. In the twilight of the cellar a curious little old woman attended to the laundry. Miss Shipp used to greet me with a wide grin that exposed a few khaki teeth and numerous gaps. Invariably she had in her apron pocket a twist of paper containing snuff, its piquancy dominating the space around her. 'What is that?' I asked. 'Snuff, dear,' she replied. 'Warms the cockles of yer 'eart.'

Tom and Mary Ann were among the most generous of people. If they heard of a case of hardship, they immediately sent aid. Mary Ann would go into the little grocer's shop of Mr Pearson, just behind their garden wall. 'Send this order to Mrs So-and-so', she said, 'but if you tell her who sent it, I'll never give you another order'. And when a poor working woman told Tom that her terminally-ill husband could not lie comfortably, and that the doctor had prescribed a water bed way beyond her means, he paid for one without hesitation.

Among some of my mother's generation there existed a certain amount of quiet cultural activity. My Auntie Connie, of a decidedly scholarly turn, spent most evenings studying French and Latin: she remained at St. Mary's Convent School until eighteen. Later, when I was in my early teens, Connie and I regularly went together to the theatre, and it was in her company that I saw my first ballet, a performance at the Arts Theatre in Cambridge by the Vic-Wells Ballet, which set me off on a lifelong interest. Connie appreciated the best things in the arts in those days, but later became almost pathologically obsessed with her religion and even attempted to take the veil; unluckily for her, she was not accepted.

My mother's eldest sibling, Jack, was an amateur painter of

considerable ability. A great lover of horses, he spent evening after evening painting studies of them in oils, several of which adorned the walls in Soham House. Another artist in oils was my mother's cousin, Dora, daughter of Great-Uncle Bill, who made some appealing landscape studies in oil colour. When about fourteen, I also tried my hand at oil painting which met with considerable derision from many of the Arnold family, who always discovered great amusement in my artistic interests, but the kind and practical Dora helped me with much valuable advice and encouragement, and Uncle Jack assured my tormentors that my attempts were not at all bad.

My youngest aunt, Ruby, dabbled from time to time in various crafts: embroidery, pictures assembled from glossy coloured adhesive paper, watercolours, and glass decorated with coloured metallic foil, backed by lacquer – a kind of primitive *verre églomisé*; she played the piano quite well and sang ballads in her pretty, but faint soprano voice. She was still at St. Mary's Convent School during my early boyhood, and in my earliest recollections of her, she wore a gym slip, and a floppy coloured silk bow in her bobbed hair. Alas! she died when only forty-seven, the first, and youngest of my mother's siblings to depart.

Great-Uncle Tom's daughter, Max, a woman of striking beauty, trained as a singer and actress and appeared, under her stage name of Mollie Nugent, in several musical comedies; this came to an end when she married. It was thrilling to me as a little boy to meet some of her actor- and actress-friends, one or two of whom from time to time stayed at her father's home. I was a great favourite of Max's who, when in Cambridge, took me about with her, and provided treats without end. Max's sister, Elsie, another beautiful woman, was an accomplished pianist, and frequently accompanied Max when she sang for the family.

Max's youngest sister, Dod, was the epitome of the 'twenties flapper; her hair was Eton cropped, and she wore a single earring, long and colourful strings of beads, skirts that finished above her knees, and she used a long and elegant jade cigarette holder. A skilful ballroom dancer, she decided to set up as a teacher, and ordered a printed leaflet to advertise her services, but its impact was somewhat subdued by her price list: five shillings (25p) for one lesson, twelve shillings (60p) for two. Although a devout Catholic, Dod rarely got the right idea and among other things remained firmly convinced that the letters R.I.P. on a memorial card stood for Rise If Possible. I liked Dod; she had inherited her parents' kindness and eccentricity, and possessed infectious and appealing laugh.

****

The somewhat protean character of the Arnolds was vividly demonstrated by the festivities at Christmas, which usually began at Soham House on Christmas Eve, with Grandad Arnold, his sons and my father visiting Great-Uncle Charlie, landlord of the Station Hotel, freely imbibing and watching him officiate at his Grand Christmas Draw, which, if the number of prizes distributed among the family was any indication, must invariably have been heavily loaded in its favour or perhaps Uncle Charlie performed sleight of hand. Even I, at five years of age, won a bottle of gin, which I fondly imagined to be a bottle of water. After this, Grandad's party returned to Soham House laden with their prizes of turkeys, whisky, gin and cigars, for further intake and fun. Sometimes the local policeman would be brought in, laced with whisky, and often persuaded to sing a song. He went out periodically, 'to meet the sergeant' as he put it, but came back as soon as possible to resume the party, always being careful to remove his helmet so that its shadow should not be silhouetted on the blind and so give the game away.

At about 11.30 my aunts got themselves ready, and set out to attend the Midnight Mass of the Nativity, and the party would break up, no doubt on being reminded of the other, more solemn aspect of the festival, far removed from the convivial pagan celebration of the winter solstice represented by the revels during the earlier part of the evening.

For my father, mother and me, Christmas Day usually began with a visit to Grandad and Granny Lister, to be followed by luncheon and the remainder of the day with my Arnold grandparents at Soham House. On Boxing Day – also my parents' wedding anniversary and my father's birthday – everybody came to our house. What rowdy and good-humoured parties they were! Christmas nowadays no longer sparks off the splendid noisy fun and richness of my childhood Christmases, when at luncheon and supper joints of pork and silverside of beef, a ham, a turkey, a huge pork pie and Christmas plum pudding would be served to twenty or more people. Drink flowed freely, and the older generation smoked cigars and played nap, while the piano tinkled away playing old favourite choruses for all to join in until they echoed through the house.

Everybody had a party piece to recite or sing: my father's was the song *Till the Sands of the Desert grow cold*; my mother's brother Jack, demobilised from the Army a few short years before, rendered *The Trumpeter*; Auntie Ruby sang *The Little Brown Owl*; and Uncle Humphrey Lant, a professional pianist who later married another of mother's sisters, Auntie Hilda, sang *Father O'Flynn*. My grandfather Arnold, sitting comfortably in his armchair beside the fireplace, smoking cigars and drinking whisky, did not sing, but loudly suggested improper song titles, which he seemed to think others might have been persuaded to render, such as *Touch 'em up while they're young, my boys*, or *Johnny up the Orchard*. Whether any of these songs actually existed I never knew, for nobody ever took up Grandad's promptings.

Apart from Christmas we often enjoyed considerable revelry at Soham House, in contrast to what always seemed a more elderly and staid atmosphere in my other grandparents' home. My father and his siblings – Auntie Maude, Auntie Bet and Uncle Alf – were an older, almost different generation from Grandad Arnold's family. My father, older than my mother, was the youngest in the Lister family, whereas my mother was the eldest in hers. Indeed two of my maternal aunts, Connie and Ruby, seemed to me more like sisters, being only fourteen and eleven years older than I. Naturally this made for a different atmosphere in each household, with more youthful high spirits and fun at Soham House, up-to-date music in the background provided by Uncle Humphrey at the pianoforte playing selections from current musical comedies such as *Lido Lady, No, No, Nanette, Rose Marie, The Desert Song*, and so on; those melodies remain very much part of my memories. But even apart from that I was fond of Uncle Humphrey, who seemed to understand the dreams of boyhood; he who presented me with my first toy theatre and, some months later, my first set of chessmen. Sometimes, the furniture would be pushed back against the wall as a prelude to energetic dancing – aunts, uncles and their friends gyrating in foxtrots, the Charleston, quicksteps and tangos to Humphrey's playing, sometimes accompanied on a Swanee whistle by another member of the family. In Uncle Humphrey's absence, a cabinet gramophone provided the music.

I suppose this very early musical background, when I was no more than six years old, must have contributed to my lifelong love of music, even if dance music of the 'twenties seems far removed from my adult tastes, which among many others, embrace the work of Mozart, Handel, Rossini, Verdi, Tchaikovsky, Mahler, Stravinsky, and above all Beethoven. When a little boy, I used to stand at the side of Uncle Humphrey while he played the piano, and pretend to conduct the music with one of Granny Arnold's knitting needles. Humphrey, as always kind and understanding of young children, told me I had an excellent sense of rhythm. Be that as it may, there has never been a period in my life when the sound of music was absent for long.

Three
A Cambridge Childhood

When I was a child my parents' home was in a bay-windowed terrace house, 66, Abbey Road, a few hundred yards from the Lister workshops. While I played in the garden I could hear the tintinnabulation of hammers on anvils. This garden formed the scene of one of my earliest memories. My mother was holding me in her arms while I watched my father fixing corrugated iron sheets to the roof of a tool-shed; I must have been less than two years old. A yard or so from this shed was the kennel of our dear old smooth-coated tricolour fox-terrier, Bob, who until I was five years old was my bosom companion. A gift to me from my mother's cousin Tom (Max's brother) when I was a baby, he was allowed to ride in my perambulator, and I often crawled into his kennel to nuzzle against him in the straw, falling asleep with him in that doggy, bony atmosphere. I am sad to say he was run over and killed by a lorry, leaving me desolate and giving me my first brush with tragedy. But Bob implanted in my breast a love of dogs that remains to this day; I cannot remember a time when I did not have at least one.

In our Abbey Road house my father indulged his hobbies, which included especially stamp collecting and wireless telegraphy. Each week, approval sheets arrived from the London philatelic dealers, Stanley Gibbons, from which he filled gaps in his album. When I was nearly seven he initiated me into the same hobby, which took hold of me to such an extent that, by the age of thirteen, I had begun to specialise in the stamps of

Great Britain, and became a proper philatelist, able to identify the work of different security printers, different papers and watermarks, and even apparently identical stamps from different printing plates. Only in early middle age did I release myself from the bondage of this pursuit.

My father's obsession with wireless was highly original, for he was one of the first people in Cambridge to own, let alone construct, a wireless receiver other than a crystal set. His creation occupied an enormous amount of space; indeed it completely filled the dining-room sideboard with accumulators, dry batteries, rows of valves and coils, and complicated wired areas, resembling the sculpture of Naum Gabo. When he was completing his first receiver, my mother told me I would soon be able to listen to Big Ben, which for some reason beyond my present comprehension I imagined to be a big Airedale terrier.

For a year or two we listened-in, as it was then expressed, with headphones, which restricted the sounds to the people wearing them – a more civilised way to enjoy broadcasting than the blaring, insistent, predatory transistor radio of the present day. As the results of the 1924 parliamentary election were broadcast, my resourceful father placed all the headphones in a silver fruit-dish to make a rudimentary loudspeaker which allowed quite a large group of people to listen together.

Children's Hour was naturally my favourite programme. Periodically it took its microphones to London Zoo, from which we could hear the cries, songs and roars of various animals and birds. In the event it was really quite disappointing, but we pretended it was all wonderful. What I really liked was the birthday programme: for a small fee, parents could have a child's name and age read on his birthday, with instructions of where he could look to find a present. My name was called at least once: 'Ray Lister is five today; he will find a present in the bookcase.' I rushed to the bookcase in the parlour, and there indeed was a parcel containing a book entitled *The Good Shepherd*, an account of the life of Jesus for children; it is still in my library.

As a little boy I possessed lots of toys; I was the first grandchild on each side of the family, and for a long time had only two cousins, so I was in consequence much spoiled. But I do not think this made me greedy or ill-natured, for I gladly gave toys to my friends; indeed my parents from time to time felt constrained to put a stop to this, but once they had forgotten, I became as open-handed as ever. Yet there were things I coveted, too. Mrs Emily Brown, our next-door neighbour, had a minute Yorkshire terrier bitch named Tiny, which I wanted dearly. One day in the garden, I reached through the dividing fence and captured her. The poor little thing must have wondered what was happening, for I shut her in my toy cupboard. A little later, Mrs Brown called round to ask my mother if she had seen the missing Tiny. With unerring intuition Mother went straight to my toy cupboard and with abject apologies returned the little bitch to her owner.

My pretty bedroom in Abbey Road overlooked our back garden. It was decorated with plain wallpaper and an attractive frieze of hounds and mounted pink-coated huntsmen setting out for a day's sport, rendered somewhat in the manner of the Beggarstaff Brothers. Over the fireplace hung a much enlarged photograph of my father as a boy of about twelve or thirteen, dressed in an Eton suit, seated beside his Old English sheepdog 'Jumbo', almost as big as himself. On other walls I recall a coloured reproduction of Dante Gabriel Rossetti's *Beata Beatrix*; a black and white lithograph by Uncle Jack of a horse drinking at a stream; and the certificate of my mother's first communion. A crucifix hung over my bed, and on the chimneypiece stood a conventional but not unattractive plaster statuette of the Virgin and Child.

This special room was my own retreat, a womb of safety within my parents' domain. It had a pleasant atmosphere, and I think that this, combined with the presence of the few artefacts, and with the pleasing diminutive designs of many of the postage stamps in my album, probably played a part in initiating my seduction by the arts.

****

My mother presided over the household with kindness, understanding and humour. A strikingly well-favoured woman, she had also a strong personality; my grandmother had left to her the upbringing of most of her children, she did most of the cooking, and when she married my father she had already experienced almost every department of household management; this meant that our Abbey Road house ran smoothly. I was loved and cherished without stint, and enjoyed numerous treats: visits to London Zoo, to the seaside, to the theatre, to mention but three.

After tea Mother sat down at the piano and played delightfully – Viennese waltzes, selections from operettas, marches, Irish melodies, and so on. Before my bedtime she would play me a pretty little piece entitled *Upstairs to Fairyland* – I have no recollection of the composer's name, even if I ever knew it.

Her cooking was marvellous, and apart from staple items like roast beef, steak and kidney pie and leg of mutton, she concocted the most succulent puddings imaginable, such as meringue cases scraped out and filled with rich whipped cream flavoured with vanilla, and the breathtaking Charlotte Royale, an amalgam of gelatine, cream, strawberry jam and strawberry syrup. And she provided cakes of all kinds: Russian roll (known elsewhere as Battenberg cake), fruit cake as rich as Christmas plum pudding, puff pastry slices stuffed with Chantilly cream and anointed with rich icing, marshmallow cake consisting of layers of sponge cake, alternating with layers of whipped cream and icing and topped with yet more icing decorated with marshmallow sweets.

If I took a friend home to a meal (they were always welcome to Mother) he gaped almost dumbfounded in admiration of the Lister table, groaning under its load of delights. My friends all loved her. She never forgot a name, never forgot their special preferences and, if she knew who was coming, his special treat would invariably be served. If one of my father's employees was working in the house, he too would be given a slice of rich creamy cake and a cup of strong tea. And if any of them ever had a sick wife or child, Mother would set to and make calf's-foot jelly, beef tea or rich egg custard, and send me to deliver them.

The thing that most upset her was injustice, so she never hesitated to tell my father if she thought he was being unnecessarily hard on anybody. Neither would she hesitate to take a complete stranger to task if she caught him doing anything sly or underhand and, if she saw evidence of bullying among young boys, they received the rough edge of her tongue.

Such was my kind and remarkable mother. I regret that religious misunderstanding came between us somewhat when I was young, but in time she did come to understand me even in that.

****

As a child I began to attend high mass every Sunday in the cathedral-like church of Our Lady and the English Martyrs in Cambridge, where I had been christened. From the beginning, the spectacle enthralled me; the Tridentine mass with its colour, its gold, its music, and above all its mystery, all as resplendent and sumptuous as grand opera. What on earth (it could not have been anything heavenly) persuaded Vatican II to replace it with the present colourless, uninspired and vernacular ceremony, I cannot even begin to guess. But even during my boyhood, a brief year or so after I began to attend church regularly, Catholic ritual and ecclesiastical dress began to lose some of their formal beauty. Priests had begun to discard the ceremonial shoes with silver buckles they had hitherto worn at the altar, apparels no longer decorated albs, the dalmatics and tunicles of the deacons lost their tassels and fringes. Yet these losses fell far short of the insipid white habits and plain chasubles like folkweave curtains worn today. As to the unimaginative vernacular of the new ritual, I remain unconvinced that, to give a brief example, 'The Lord be with you' – 'And with you', is as dignified or as convincing as 'Dominus vobiscum' – 'Et cum spiritu tuo'.

Doubtless those who like and support the new ritual will claim that the loss of certain types of dress and words has nothing to do with religious truth. I do not agree; much can be said in favour of numinous ceremonial for the dramatic presentation of religious mystery. One could really believe during the canon of the old mass, amid twinkling sanctuary lamps, hazy incense and coruscating candles, that some great event was taking place, that a deity was in truth present. At the similar point in the new ritual, the priest, facing the congregation, has about as much spiritual and imaginative appeal as a market stallholder.

The Catholic Church provides refuge for many oddities, not the least of whom was Miss Eva Webster, a teacher at the

25

Catholic Primary School and a dedicated lay worker, who came to our house once a week, to instruct me in catechism and to prepare me for confirmation. Admittedly I was very young, but I was not unintelligent, and I think I might have been treated with somewhat more respect than to be told that the letters IHS stood for 'I have suffered', and that if I ever dared to cast aside the Catholic faith I should at death be despatched to Hell to spend eternity in perpetual torment. Worse, when I asked to be told the difference between mortal and venial sin, Miss Webster defined it thus: 'It would be a mortal sin if you were to steal five shillings (25p); a smaller sum would probably be considered venial'. And when I asked the dear old soul what would happen to me if I were to commit the mortal sin of peculating five shillings, she said that when I died, I would go to Hell, and when I arrived there, everybody would laugh at me.

I felt troubled that, according to Webster, Protestants were by no means certain to achieve Paradise. I thought of my beloved father and my dear old Baptist grandfather: and asked with considerable anxiety, 'Would they *never* go to Heaven?' 'Oh, perhaps after *many* centuries,' she said, with unction, 'after whole ages in Purgatory.' It will surprise few, if any, of my readers, that at her sixth visit, I ran out of the back door as she arrived at the front, and flatly refused to see her. She never returned and, doubtless due to my father's influence (for which I am grateful), I questioned religious dogmas more and more as I grew older – much more than even he approved, for at heart he remained a deeply convinced Christian.

Other religious influences added puzzlement during my childhood. My father constantly and pertinaciously made sure that I became aware of other views; for instance he sometimes took me to Protestant services. At the same time he himself took a deep interest in the occult and attended spiritualist séances (he never took me to these), and magazines such as *Psyche* ; books, among which were Sir Oliver Lodge's *Raymond* (1916) and Nea Walker's *The Bridge* (1927); and treatises, on such subjects as the symbolism of the Great Pyramid, arrived almost every week. I heard much talk and discussion of the survival of the human soul after death, an idea that seemed pleasant enough to me, but most of our Catholic relations disapproved of such speculation, though if anything that made my father more persistent in his investigations. Later in life he concluded that some psychical phenomena were genuine, but that they were potentially dangerous and best left alone. As for my mother, while remaining a Catholic at heart, she said little, but I am afraid my own religious rebelliousness upset her: she felt particularly displeased when I gave my rosary for a necklace to a pretty little crippled girl who lived nearby.

****

Our district enjoyed plenty of entertainment, especially circuses and fairs. Of circuses, the usual visitor during the 1920s was that of 'Lord' George Sanger, but in the 1930s Bertram Mills's Circus and some others paid regular visits. Each of these attracted me like a needle to so many magnets: I adored their colour and bustle.

A little farther afield, on Jesus Green, the 'Mammoth Show', a fair-cum-county-show launched by local enterprise, was held during August. It included a fun-fair, sporting events, livestock competitions, a firework display and a balloon ascent with parachute jumps: one year a girl parachutist was killed when her 'chute caught on a bridge. As for the fireworks, when I was little I simply *hated* the rockets, which flew up too far and brought on what became a pathological fear of heights; I could not have been very old, for I was in a pushchair, which my mother turned around with the hood up, to hide the offending display from my sight. Despite my horror of rockets I was not disturbed by the stars, and on my way home that evening, I asked my mother if they were made by Jesus punching holes in the floor of heaven so that its light shone through.

The most memorable event of the year's round of entertainment and one I always anticipated with almost uncontrolled excitement was the big Midsummer Fair, held on Midsummer Common towards the end of June, and opened officially by the Mayor of Cambridge attended by the Town Clerk, Common Cryer and Macebearer, all in full civic panoply. After the ceremony, a few (*very* few) new pennies were thrown among the crowd by the Mayor. Midsummer Fair still continues, but the present fair with its jazzed-up rides and blaring loudspeakers spewing pop music cannot compare with its more romantic predecessors of the 1920s and 1930s, during the days of spectacular switchbacks. Described somewhat optimistically by their proprietors as 'scenic railways', they were large carousels with cars in the form of dragons, peacocks, dolphins, motor-cars, whales or Venetian gondolas, which travelled on rails in a circle, on ascending and descending inclines. The whole structure was encrusted with elaborate carving, gesso, paint, etched and cut glass and polished brass. Originally powered by steam engines, by the 1920s the most up-to-date rides were electric. Most beautiful was the Peacock Park, a magnificent example of fairground baroque: its cars, giant peacocks with illuminated eyes, were upholstered in velvet and seated about ten or twelve people apiece.

Within the central area of this switchback stood a huge mechanical organ, mounted with carved figures with moving arms and heads; the principal one, at the centre, was a toreador in a suit of lights, conducting the music. In front of the organ stood a desk in a small cabin, where the showman received the fares from men who, to collect them, jumped on to the moving cars. But the most delightful of all the decorative features on this great roundabout stood at the back of the organ: a pool with scagliola steps rising above it on three sides, down which cascaded a real waterfall, with coloured electric lights beneath. It might have been, or may have been derived from, a folk recollection of the cascades at the Villa d'Este at Tivoli. It was my favourite ride and I rode on it as often as I had enough money, or as often as I could persuade anybody to treat me. Steam traction-engines provided major attractions at pre-war fairs: decorated almost as splendidly as the roundabouts, with bright paint, coloured electric lights and polished brass, twisted like sticks of sugar-candy, they bore imposing names, spelled out in brass letters riveted to the boiler casing, such as 'King George V', and 'Admiral Beatty'. Usually, when the fair was travelling in our part of the country, one or more of them, and working parts of the rides, would be brought into the Lister workshops for service or repair.

These fairground sideshows transported one into a fantasy

world: fat women, marionettes, lion-tamers, pugilists, midgets, and many more, including especially dancing girls who imparted something of the 'naughty 'nineties', for these fairground entertainments were always more or less *passés*, and none the worse for it. Typical were a pimply little girl in briefs reclining among small pythons, and described on the placard outside the booth as an oriental beauty lying among venomous snakes in constant peril of her life; and a young woman, dressed only in a bathing costume, reclining on a mat in a casing made of blocks of ice, shivering, or pretending to shiver, nonchalantly smoking a cigarette, and advertised as a beauty encased in ice. And there I recall 'Tiny Tim' the midget: a minute carriage and diminutive articles of clothing were displayed outside his booth. He was really tiny, the size of a twelve-months old baby, and could stand on the showman's hand. Poor little creature! If ever a freak suffered exploitation, it was he. As we filed into the quiet booth (booths always seemed quiet after the chatter and clamour of the surrounding fairground) he sat on a stool in the corner of a railed-off area. He looked at us, uncomprehending and bad-tempered, shouting incoherently. The showman came in, said his piece, and asked Tiny Tim what he would like to drink. 'Dinnits', said the midget, perhaps meaning Guinness. The showman then told us that Tim would sell us his life story, printed on one side of a single small sheet of paper, price one penny. Now the little fellow smiled and to each person who bought a copy, he said 'Ta', like a baby.

The shows usually proved a disappointment and the outside spectacle would almost invariably be more interesting than anything to be seen inside. Most amusing were the barkers, who addressed the crowds, urging them to enter the booth and see the show. One I remember performing conjuring tricks; a bare-legged girl stood at his side: 'Watch closely, ladies and gentlemen', he said, 'while I pass this potato through the young lady's "Little Mary"!' In front of another booth, the gathering crowd was regaled by a row of dancing girls in grubby costumes, consisting mainly of tassels and little else. When their dance had ended the barker, a greasy, curly-haired and corpulent young man in a dinner suit, with a multi-coloured ribbon across his chest, spoke these works in a strong Italian accent:

'Ladies an' gentlemen. In-a dis show you see-a everythink. It is a-guarantee to leave-a nothink to de imagination. We not only show you the bodies of dese-a beautiful young ladies, but you shall see every goose-a pimple!' That was enough. Half a dozen callow youths with cigarettes drooping from the corners of their mouths, thrust their hands into their pockets, walked up to the pay-desk and laid down their sixpences. The Italian barker soon had his full house.

There were many further attractions: ice-cream vendors, fortune-tellers (each one claiming to be 'the original' Madame this or Gypsy that), crockery auctioneers, shellfish bars, toy dealers and vendors of rock and nougat, including the *soi-disant* 'Rock King', James Arthur Lewin, from Peterborough, who wore a two-gallon hat, a tartan tie and loud check suit with riding-breeches and leggings. Even more memorable was the skinny beldam in charge of the latrines, who called attention to the service she offered by proclaiming at the top of her voice, 'Piddle and poop a penny!'

****

Further interest was available when we ventured as far as Market Hill at the centre of Cambridge, which is not a hill, but a flat, square area, named perhaps on the same principle as the May Week celebrations of the University colleges, which last a fortnight and are held in June.

The market provided entertainment to us children in the form of a splendid Punch and Judy show set up every Saturday opposite Bacon's famous tobacco shop: it belonged to and was operated by Mr. George Rose of King's Lynn. The puppets were magnificent Italian artefacts, hand-carved, fitted with glass eyes, and elaborately dressed – Punch and Joey the clown were arrayed in splendid attire derived from the *Commedia dell'Arte*. The libretto (based on the 1828 version by John Payne Collier) contained many street-corner vulgarities and much knockabout, like any Punch show worthy of its tradition. Puritans claim that this was unfit for children. I disagree; I saw it often enough and loved it, and do not think I suffered any ill effects. It may even have provided a safety valve, harmlessly and vicariously working off potentially dangerous aggressive tendencies. It marked a sad day for English children when Punch disappeared from the street corner.

The old Guildhall, overlooking the market, was a somewhat dull brick building, though not so dull as the one that replaced it in the 1930s and still lumbers the townscape. It had a cast iron arcade with a glazed roof, and beneath this assembled daily the strangest collection of characters one could ever see in one place. There must have been around a dozen of them, but the three who come to mind at once were known as 'The Three Graces of Cambridge': 'Sluice' Parker, 'Lightning' and 'Oakey'. They, and stories of them, enlivened my childhood years. 'Sluice' Parker's nickname was derived from his sibilant lisp which recalled the sound of water rushing through a sluice-gate. He perambulated Cambridge selling flowers from a little basket which was slung over his arm. He was as cunning as a fox: one of his tricks was to remove a pot plant from a front garden, take it to the back door and say to the lady of the house: 'Lovely plant, mum. It will match the one you've got in the front garden.' It is surprising how often he succeeded in repeating this. He was called to the colours during the Great War, but got his discharge from the Army within the first week after trying to sell postcards to the colonel, so who is to say he was a fool?

'Sluice' undertook odd gardening jobs, such as the maintenance of window boxes at undergraduates' lodgings. A first-year undergraduate at Jesus College, who at this stage of his career remained innocent of Sluice's methods, asked him to plant his window boxes with tulips. Plant them he did, and in spring time the bulbs grew vigorously – into shallots. The not unnaturally incensed client complained about this when he next saw 'Sluice', who, never at a loss, asked him, 'Did you water them with cold water or 'ot?' 'Cold, of course.' 'Ah,' said 'Sluice' with a knowing wink. 'No wonder they've come up as shallots. You should 'ave used 'ot water, sir.'

'Sluice' did have a positive side so far as I was concerned, for when I was a tiny boy mother bought plants from him – daisies, pansies, petunias – and a trowel from a nearby shop, and gave me a small area of garden to cultivate. I found this a delight, but as so often in my later life, my enthusiasm outran my judgement, for when some workmen left a tin of tar in the garden after repairing a fence, it occurred to me that the daffodils would be enhanced by a liberal application of the liquid, with disastrous results to my gardening career.

'Lightning' – his real name was Siggers – was a newspaper vendor who at times wore an old Etonian tie, donated by a jocular undergraduate. He walked the streets grasping a placard and a handful of newspapers. Always topical, on Armistice Day he wore a tin hat, and during May Week, a straw boater decorated with a ribbon of First and Third Trinity or Lady Margaret boat clubs. During a particularly long heatwave he was seen carrying a placard bearing the legend: 'ICEBERG SIGHTED IN THE NORTH SEA'. 'Lightning' was a great favourite among generations of undergraduates, with whom he was always ready to exchange badinage, and from which he rarely emerged as the vanquished party. He had two very respectable sisters who ran a hairdressing salon at the corner of Bridge and St. John's Streets.

'Oakey' was a mild-looking little man clothed in an old macintosh and a battered felt hat, giving the impression, as it were, of a poor man's E.M. Forster. A pair of timid light blue eyes peered through steel-framed glasses with thick lenses, above a bedraggled blond moustache. He specialised in conducting transatlantic visitors on tours of the colleges, and being asked by one of them who built King's College Chapel, 'Oakey' took an old memorandum book from his pocket, turned over one or two grubby pages and said, 'Rattee and Kett'. Rattee and Kett is a Cambridge firm responsible for the creation and maintenance of many fine buildings, but as it was not founded until the nineteenth century it can hardly have had anything to do with the erection of Henry VI's chapel. Nevertheless the Americans seemed satisfied, as indeed they did soon afterwards when their conductor pointed to the spot in Trinity Great Court where he claimed, Queen Elizabeth I was beheaded.

Two ex-servicemen organ grinders circled around the market in the early 1920s, one of them accompanying the player of the street-piano with two pairs of clattering spoons which he played up and down his arms like castanets. Stalls were also run by butchers, corn-cure experts, haberdashers, purveyors of sweets and rock, florists, fishmongers and fruiterers. On a winter's evening it resembled a nocturne painted by Atkinson Grimshaw, together with noisy bustle and pungent smells mingled with the aroma of naphtha flares, thoughts of which will never fail to yield memories of childhood evenings with my parents on visits to the town centre.

****

The children who lived in and around Abbey Road, like all town children, had a repertoire of street games. I thought it more adventurous to play in the street than in the seclusion of our garden. My parents disapproved and I could only join in if I escaped by stealth; thus street games had for me the added attraction of forbidden fruit. Periodic crazes arose for various games: whiptop, hoops, kites and marbles all came into vogue at different seasons of the year. Cigarette cards always stayed in fashion, and we unashamedly gambled for each other's duplicates. To do this we leaned a row of cards against a wall, and took turns to flick other cards at them. If he knocked a card down, the lucky player took all that were lying there, including any previously unsuccessful flicked cards. Sometimes as many as thirty or forty cards might at one throw be won in this way.

We also played such games as tig, hide-and-seek, hopscotch and leapfrog. Many of these games demanded that one should be 'it' – the player who hid, or started off games like tig – and this was determined by a counting-out rhyme:

Eeny, meeny, miny, mo,
Ah, vah, vector,
Thou shalt not be it.

Skipping remained a popular pastime, and a spectacular display took place not far from our home every Good Friday, when hordes of children, many accompanied by their parents, descended on Parker's Piece, a big open park, and spent the day skipping and picnicking. By midday the Piece was full of skippers, with food vendors' stalls, and hot cross buns much in evidence around the perimeter.

Games in our garden were commonly more elaborate than street games. When either the circus or the fair arrived we children had our own make-believe fair or circus in the garden. After elaborate preparations in which old boxes, planks of wood and garden seats would be arranged as roundabouts, slides or auditoria, other children were invited in to have 'rides' or to watch a performance. When Auntie Ruby's future husband gave me a set of Punch and Judy puppets with carved-wood heads, my father built me a smart booth against the garden fence. It really seemed to me quite professional and I had no difficulty in finding several large audiences from among children in the neighbourhood. I am sure such activities contained the seeds that germinated into my lifelong love of the theatre.

I also presented my show of 'Cheddar Gorge' in our garden. My mother and father had taken me to the original Gorge during an early summer holiday in 1926, at the time of the General Strike. I remember that the dicky seat of my father's Swift motor-car was piled up with cans of petrol, in case supplies ran out. We visited the famous caves with their stalactites and stalagmites which so impressed me that I decided to have a cave of my own after we had returned. So I set it up in the roost of an old chicken house at the bottom of the garden. Small heaps of old bricks and tiles represented the stalagmites – I could not have stalactites as I could find no way to fix the bricks to the roof. Dripping water was supplied by old tin cans with holes knocked in their bottoms, which I placed on shelves. It was pitch dark and I took tremulous visiting children in one at a time to admire the beauties by the light of an electric torch.

Whenever we had pennies to spend on chocolate and sweets, we could make our purchases at many small local shops. Some of them even made their own stock, and among these were the shops of the Reynolds family who called themselves 'Rock Kings', in rivalry with Lewin of Peterborough. The Reynoldses made and sold fragrant old-fashioned boiled sweets, nougat, sticks of rock, toffee-apples and brandy-snaps rarely, if ever, seen elsewhere.

More conventional stock could be found in the little sweet and tobacco shop of Harold Missen, a mild little man like a bald version of Charlie Chaplin. He was the butt of innumerable practical jokes, many of them perpetrated by my mother's brothers and cousins. Once, when he was decorating his shop window, my Uncle Jack and Cousin George stealthily shot the bolt, locking him in where he stood, while he gesticulated wildly, yelling imprecations, as Jack and George wanted, and they quickly called a crowd together, saying 'Look! Missen's gone mad!' They then walked off, leaving him to his own devices.

****

Such was the colourful and entertaining ambience in which I grew up: there is now nothing to resemble it. Education, television and wireless have all contributed to its demise, and in many ways that is a good thing. There are now no barefoot children walking the streets, as there were when I was a child. Housing is better and there is less disease. There are far fewer illiterates than then.

If my grandparents were to be resurrected they would hardly recognise their district, with its new roads, new blocks of flats, new warehouses and workshops. It cannot be disputed that it has lost much of its attractive and interesting character, but it is cleaner underfoot, even if such cleanliness is somewhat subverted by air pollution from exhaust fumes.

Four
My Three Schools

*

Soon after my fifth birthday in 1924, I began to attend what may
be best described as a glorified dame-school, presided over by
Miss Emma Royston, a forbidding old lady of disagreeable visage and skinny stature. Rather grandly, she called it St Clair
School, from the name of its premises, a house on Newmarket
Road, close to Christ Church, Ambrose Poynter's red-brick pastiche of King's College Chapel. Nobody else ever used the
school's formal name: to the world at large it was always 'Miss
Royston's'. It catered for the education of boys up to about the
age of eight, when they would be ready to move on to a preparatory school, and girls up to the age of sixteen. My Aunts Connie
and Ruby had been among Miss Royston's pupils some years
previously, before progressing to higher education under the
nuns at Paston House in Bateman Street.

Miss Royston was assisted by Miss Blanche Stonebridge,
whose father worked as a clerk at the Star Brewery, on the opposite side of Newmarket Road, the pungent aroma from which
permeated the school on brewing days. Sometimes during
classes, a girl from the main schoolroom would come into what
was called 'the babies' room' for pianoforte lessons, which were
an 'extra', Miss Stonebridge continually exhorting her pupil to
'mind your fingers'. Instruction in the French language, another
'extra', was imparted to older children by a tall, middle-aged
spinster named Humm.

During the evening, Miss Royston provided dancing lessons

for suitable young ladies, instructing them in the elegances of the waltz and such formal dances as *Sir Roger de Coverly* and quadrilles. She even went so far as to initiate her pupils into the mysteries of the polka, but further than that she refused to budge: the foxtrot, the quickstep, to say nothing of the Charleston, were obnoxious to her.

The physical education of the scholars was not taken seriously, but some obeisance was made to it once a week, when we were marched to the nearby church hall, in which we were put through a gentle form of drill with wooden hand-dumb-bells. This alternated with songs with gestures, accompanied by Miss Stonebridge at the piano. One such song was:

Oats and beans and barley grow,
Oats and beans and barley grow,
But not you nor I nor anyone know,
How oats and beans and barley grow.

First the farmer sows his seed,
Then he stands and takes his ease,
Stamps his feet and claps his hand
And turns around and views the land.

Such dance and song games were popular at the children's parties arranged by our parents. We never tired of *Here we come gathering nuts in May, Oranges and Lemons say the Bells of St Clement's*, or of games like *Hunt the Thimble, I Spy*, and *This is my Friend's Seat*. I wonder how many children still know them?

My special debt to Miss Stonebridge, a gifted teacher of young children, is that she taught me to read – one of the most valuable gifts any human being can bestow on another. By the age of six I could read quite fluently, and it proved a great resource when a year later, in 1926, I was struck down with diphtheria, caught from our housemaid, and was consigned to the local fever hospital for several weeks. My father arranged for comic papers to be delivered to me every day: *Tiger Tim's Weekly, Bubbles, Sunbeam, Rainbow, Playbox*, and many more, the perusal of which helped me, when I had recovered a little, to pass what would otherwise have been insupportable dreariness.

My incarceration began on November 1, which meant that I should be in hospital on Guy Fawkes' Day, and so miss the usual bonfire and fireworks. The hospital sister very kindly brought the children some sparklers which she lighted and held for them, so they were not completely deprived. I enjoyed my sparklers alone, for I was in a private ward; I did not mind this at all, for even as a child I was fairly self-sufficient. But pangs of homesickness sometimes took charge of me, especially when I heard the children in the big ward singing:

> Mother, mother, take me home
> From the sanatorium.
> If I stay a week or two,
> Will you take me home with you?

I found most of the nursing staff very pleasant and kind, but once a week the regular sister had a day off duty, to be replaced by a sister from the nearby scarlet fever hospital, an unmitigated bully both to the staff and to the child patients. A young nurse, herself convalescing from diphtheria, occasionally read to me, before I felt well enough to read myself. If she did this when the temporary sister was on duty, that lady would look round the door with a Mephistophelean scowl, curling her moustachioed lips, while she barked, 'Nurse! Get on with your work!' At this my friend would disappear, intimidated for the remainder of the day. If visiting-day happened to coincide with this charmer's turn of duty, she would come into my ward with an ill-humoured visage, and say, 'If your parents bring you any gifts you are not to unwrap them.' I was terrified of her, and almost equally terrified of the matron, a big, stiff, pugnacious lowland Scot with a reproachful voice. Dr. Ernest Lloyd Jones, our physician, described her as a 'treetrunk in nurse's uniform'.

At the end of five weeks, I was declared free of infection and discharged. When I reached home, I discovered that my parents had put aside a supply of fireworks for a special display a day or two later, which I watched from my bedroom window, and Alfie Brown the little boy next door watched from his.

When I first went to school, my mother took me to and fro each morning and afternoon, but after about a year she considered it safe enough for me to walk the few hundred yards to Soham House, from where one of my aunts would see me safely across the busy Newmarket Road. On the whole a child could walk the streets in those days with little fear of molestation, but one day I did receive a horrid fright. I had been seen across the road and was quietly making my way to school, when a dirty and ragged old crone slightly ahead of me turned around, and with a face distorted by animosity, beckoned me energetically and screamed in a blood-curdling voice, 'Come 'ere! Come 'ere!' Some women standing in a cottage doorway called to me: 'Cross the road, sonny!' I did better than that, and fled back to Soham House in terror. My Auntie Connie then saw me safely all the way to school, but I was still shaking with terror, imagining how the old woman could have kidnapped me, and that I might never again have seen my parents. Though probably perfectly harmless, deranged perhaps since her menopause, or perhaps by drink, I thought her really horrendous. My terror was somewhat increased by my mother's opinion that she was 'off her head', by which I imagined that somehow her head had become separated from her body and had been rejoined to it by a broomstick stuck into the separated parts of her neck – in much the same way that I repaired my toy soldiers by putting a matchstick into their severed necks.

****

By March 1927 I was eight, and my father removed me from Miss Royston's and sent me as a day boy to St John's College Choir School, which was then in All Saints' Passage behind the Hawks' Club, in the centre of Cambridge; its origins dated from the 17th century. I was not a member of the choir: choirboys received free education in return for their services to the College, and wore Eton suits with big stiff collars and bum-freezer jackets. The other pupils who, like me, paid fees, wore flannel trousers and blazers. I doubt that this sartorial segregation was a good thing; the near-uniforms of the choristers did smack somewhat of charity schools with their often absurd costumes, like those of the Charitable Grinders in *Dombey and Son*, although I must admit that I was at the time innocent of such considerations; but what, I wonder, were the feelings of the choristers?

The Master in Charge, the Reverend Sam Senior M.A. (Cantab.), a plump, cherubic little parson, stood little more than five feet tall, soberly dressed in correct cloth, far removed from the sartorial preferences of the present-day parson, which often consist of nothing more than a clerical collar worn with sports clothes or even jeans and a pullover. Though strict, he maintained on the whole good-humoured discipline, reinforced at times by a restrained use of the cane – one stroke across the palm of the hand being the usual limit, although for heinous offences there would be one on each hand, but that was unusual.

At heart Sam was a thoroughly decent man, and I am glad to say he remained a good friend of our family until he died many years after my schooldays. When we married, my wife and I both decided that nobody but Sam should conduct the ceremony, and later he baptised each of our children. As a teacher, he impressed us by example, as for instance when many of the boys admitted never having tasted junket, he got May, his housemaid, to make a large dish of it, from which each of us enjoyed a taste. And he introduced original elements into the school curriculum, such as a curious recital of passages from Shakespeare by a very old white-haired clergyman, Canon Edward Curtis Baldwin from nearby Harston, who sat concealed behind a screen and declaimed, with every dramatic vocal resource, whole scenes from *The Merchant of Venice, Othello* and *Macbeth*. To assist our imagination, every chink of light from the windows was blacked out, and we had to put our heads down on the desks, our hands covering our eyes, so that we were in complete darkness. It all seemed very sinister, especially in the more dramatic and blood-curdling passages. Some time back, I was pleasantly surprised to read in Mr Graham Greene's memoirs, *A Sort of Life* (London, 1971), that he too remembered this little man and his Shakespearean *tour-de-force*. At the beginning of one term, Sam introduced a pet jackdaw in the school yard in a large cage with an ever-open door. Sam used Jack's presence as a device to introduce us to all kinds of jackdaw references and allusions in literature and in natural history studies, from R.H. Barham's 'Jackdaw of Rheims' in his *Ingoldsby Legends* to Thomas Bewick's *History of British Birds*. The fate of Jack eludes me; perhaps, like so many pet jackdaws, he drowned himself.

At St John's we launched into Latin and French in our first term, and for the rest our education mainly comprised a simple regime of scripture and the three Rs, which included weekly readings, each pupil in turn reading a paragraph or two from works such as *The Pilgrim's Progress* and Lew Wallace's *Ben Hur* (1880), the film of which was then being shown at the Playhouse Cinema in Mill Road. On our term's report, no marks or position in class were given, only a brief assessment of the pupil's performance in each subject, such as 'excellent' (this was rare), 'very good', 'good' and so on, down to 'very weak'. At the end of the report, Sam would enlarge somewhat on this; my usual appraisal was: 'Raymond is intelligent, but pays insufficient attention.' Little wonder when there were so many really interesting things to occupy my mind, from stamp collecting and Red Indian stories to my most recent visit to the cinema or to the theatre.

We had no examinations. Instead, at the end of each term we answered what Sam called 'tests'. I think he must have considered that the word 'examination' was a frightener, and to some extent this was true. The simple tests merely discovered how much of the term's studies we had retained. And there were no prizes; instead, each boy, whatever his age, whether his work or behaviour were good or bad, was given a Christmas gift on the last day of the Michaelmas Term. In 1927 each of us received a handsome ebony hairbrush and comb, and in 1928 we were given decorated tins of toffees. It was much better than a system of prizes, which would have favoured only those who were facile at answering examination questions – not necessarily a corollary to intelligence or ability if the subsequent CVs of some prizewinners at my later school are evidence.

Sam Senior was a firm believer in the educational value of travel, and every two years or so took a party of his boys abroad. Just before I joined the school there had been a visit to Spain, and during my time, there was a visit to Holland; my parents at first decided that I should join the party, but this was prevented by illness. However, not to be outshone, I boasted to the other boys that I had been to Australia. Soon after this, during a geography lesson, Sam asked if any boy could point out on the wall map the biggest island in the world. I, rushing in where angels fear to tread, put up my hand, walked over to the map and placed my finger on Australia.

'Quite right', said Sam.

'He's been there', cried several boys, whom I would gladly have throttled.

'Have you?' asked Sam delightedly. 'You must tell us about it one day. How long did you stay there?'

'A fortnight', I lied unashamedly, determined not to lose face with the other boys.

The dénouement came some weeks later, when Sam was discussing me with my father. 'He has travelled widely, hasn't he?' said Sam.

'He has been to most parts of England'.

'But he told me he had been to Australia!'

My father quickly disabused him, and I must say that Sam took it very well; he was always amused by boyish fantasy. But it did not prevent him from spreading the good news soon afterwards by asking me in front of the whole school: 'Now Lister, when exactly *did* you visit Australia?'

'I have never been there, sir'

Sam grinned. 'But he *told* us he had, didn't he, boys?' The ensuing peals of laughter must have been the most mortifying I ever endured.

One further episode cured me of boasting for ever. A friend of Granny Arnold had given me her grown-up son's discarded stamp collection, which contained a fine used specimen of the handsome 1 rupee 50 cents rose from the 1899 issue for Ceylon. It was then valued in Stanley Gibbons's catalogue at fifteen shillings (75p), a fortune to a young schoolboy whose pocket money amounted to no more than a shilling (5p) a week. 'I have a stamp worth fifteen shillings', I boasted to other collectors in my form. Their reaction, no doubt remembering the Australian episode, was risible disbelief. I did not argue, but decided to prove my boast by demonstration. So I carefully removed the stamp from my album, put it into an envelope, and showed it to the doubters, who gasped with envy. Having triumphantly proved my point I forgot all about my treasure until a few days later I tore up what I thought was an unwanted envelope I found in my pocket. It contained, need I add, the Ceylon stamp with its corner ripped off: the gods had taken appropriate revenge for my hubris.

On two mornings the main schoolroom would be taken over during the first period for choir practice under the direction of a very tart character, Dr. Cyril B. Rootham, director of music at St John's College, and President of the Cambridge University Music Society. He was also incidentally an uncle of Edith Sitwell's governess and later companion, Helen Rootham. The choristers were very wary of him, but he did for many years knock the choir into shape as one of the best college ensembles in Cambridge.

Sam's principal assistant was his wife, Miriam, who instructed us in arithmetic, English composition and dictation. He also employed a few visiting teachers, including Mrs. Bass, a Frenchwoman married to an Englishman and resident in Cambridge; she endeavoured to impart colloquial French to us. It was a good idea, but her method was haphazard, her voice shrill, her personality excitable, and more often than not, her classes disintegrated into delightful chaos. One or two undergraduates from St John's College, reading for the church or for teaching, also lent a hand. Among them was a nephew of the Rev. 'Pat' McCormick, the famous Great War army chaplain, and later vicar of St Martin-in-the-Fields in London. This nephew, Joseph Conybeare McCormick, later also a clergyman, supervised our games on the College playing fields, which despite the fact that I shared my desk with Leonard Halls, a nephew of the great cricketer, Jack Hobbs, I loathed, never came to tolerate, yet alone love, and which I still abominate.

My father did his best to transform me into a sportsman; he even went so far as to buy me a cricket bat which was the envy of the other boys (it was later purloined by one of them), an expensive football and a pair of boxing gloves. As to boxing, I really could not (and still cannot) see the point of a sport that almost inevitably leads to hurt or injury of one kind or another. Cricket and football, though comparatively harmless, seemed to me utterly pointless, and in truth nothing to get worked up about. One of the main drawbacks in organised team sports is that they play into the hands of humourless hearties whose bullying propensities develop into harassment of those forced to take part in what they see as unmitigated boredom. Of course I know of exceptions: C.B. Fry was one of the most civilised of men, and Neville Cardus proved as apt in music as in cricket. I might perhaps have become interested in such single-handed sports as archery, fencing, or perhaps even sculling – but team sports such as rugby, soccer and cricket never! I was not cut out to be *homo ludens*.

Sam suffered serious illness during part of my second year at St John's, and a temporary headmaster was engaged. Mr Wilson was younger than Sam and, if more devoted to the cane, was nevertheless in other ways more up-to-date in his views on education. He it was who first introduced me to *Alice's Adventures in Wonderland*, to Mark Twain's *Tom Sawyer*, and to Kipling's *Jungle Books*. More generally, he induced the whole school to enthusiastically assemble a scrapbook of contemporary newspaper and magazine clippings. For the first time in the school's history, older boys were introduced to the elements of physics and chemistry. Whether Sam allowed this to continue after his return I do not know, for by then I had moved on.

So far as my own development is concerned, the most important of all Sam's visiting teachers was Albert Cousins, who once a week gave us a lesson in calligraphy and in the illumination of manuscripts; an anachronism no doubt in the England of 1927, but one which caught my imagination, and indicated, however mistily, my first step in the art of miniature painting. Among the gems brought to my attention by Cousins was William Blake's *Songs of Innocence*, for we had to write out 'The Lamb', and decorate it with a tiny roundel of the *Agnus Dei* standing in a flowery mead. Both poem and decoration appealed to me, and from that day until the present I do not recall a period during which I was not conscious of Blake's work.

Cousins left about a year after my first term at St John's to take a post on the warding staff of the Fitzwilliam Museum, then under the direction of his mentor, Sydney Carlyle Cockerell. Soon after he started there, I visited the Museum with another boy. Cousins seemed delighted to see us: 'Now', he said, 'I'll show you boys some *real* illuminating', and conducted us to some cases in the Lower Marlay Gallery, in which were displayed some manuscript fragments, elaborately illuminated and decorated with miniatures, far richer than I could ever have imagined.

The Fitzwilliam seemed an Aladdin's cave to me, full of treasures and marvels. Although its full potentialities evaded me for some years, I had in fact been there some time before Cousins took up his job. When nearly eight years old, I had been taken by my father to see our family physician, Dr. Ernest Lloyd Jones, about a skin eruption on my face. Lloyd Jones's consulting rooms were in Trumpington Street, and half an hour after he had finished with me, while we were waiting for an ointment he had prescribed to be made up at Peck's the chemist nearby, my father proposed a brief visit to the Museum opposite. I do not really recall much of that visit, except that I pored over a display case full of antique jewelled and enamelled watches, and inspected a richly gilded and painted *cassone* which even now stands in the same place in the Upper Marlay Gallery. But it was at least a beginning, and it would be impossible to exaggerate the importance of the Museum throughout my life and work; it has opened new vistas, and has allowed me to dwell on almost every aspect of the visual arts, in an ambience which comes close to that of a beautiful country house. For the floors were covered with rare oriental carpets and rugs, with fine furniture imaginatively placed, and with bowls and vases of splendid flower arrangements everywhere. Without uniformed attendants, there was nothing institutional about it, and so it remains.

****

To my father's credit, my home education became at least as important as my instruction at school. Although he almost lost his sight when working on torpedoes during the Great War, and in consequence had to read with the assistance of a strong magnifying glass, he was a firm believer in Carlyle's dictum that 'The true university of these days is a collection of books.' He therefore ensured that I had plenty of books, and among other things, even before I could read he subscribed to the periodical issues on sale in 1922-25 of Arthur Mee's *Children's Encyclopedia* (first published in 1908) which, as each volume was completed, he had bound in handsome blue cloth. He loaned each of these in turn to

Grandad Lister, who read it from cover to cover. Later our shelves also contained the same editor's *Children's Treasure House* (1926-28) and the pictorial dictionary *I See All* (1928-30), even now still a useful work of reference. Mee's periodicals *The Children's Newspaper* (founded in 1919) and *My Magazine* (founded in 1926) were always in the house.

When I was about ten or twelve my father gave me three more books edited by Mee: *The Children's Bible* (1924) and the anthologies *One Thousand Beautiful Things* (1925) and *The Book of Everlasting Things* (1927). These two anthologies first introduced me to much in the mainstream of English literature, including among many others, the works of Tennyson, Byron, Milton and Shakespeare; especially they reinforced the attractions of William Blake, for they not only printed selections from his poetry, but also George Richmond's evocative letter to Samuel Palmer, describing Blake's death as he sang songs of praise for the visions he was vouchsafed of Heaven.

All the works Arthur Mee edited bore the unmistakable stamp of his limitations and prejudices, yet generally speaking they did much to animate enthusiasms in children of my generation. True, he was guilty of wild distortions, as when he described Blake as 'our little man of dreams' – how Blake would have raged! – and he had a strong prejudice against alcohol, so much so that it is a little surprising that my father decided to give me his books, for everybody in the family enjoyed a drink. No doubt Father thought that Mee's prejudice was better than its opposite.

My lighter childhood reading (if reading it may be called) included the adventures of Pip, Squeak and Wilfred in *The Daily Mirror*. These appeared in strip cartoons, drawn by Austin B. Payne, and printed on a children's page presided over by 'Uncle Dick' (B.J. Lamb); the principal (anthropomorphic) characters were Pip (a dog of indeterminate provenance), Squeak (a penguin) and Wilfred (a rabbit with enormously elongated ears). Of the many incidental characters I remember best Squeak's Auntie, a resourceful but somewhat disreputable, one might say Bohemian, old penguin, who from time to time became involved with Popski, a 'Bolshy hound' complete with beard, whose master Wtzkoffski never tired of his predictably unsuccessful attempts to blow up or kidnap Pip, Squeak and Wilfred. These convincing, indeed inspired, cartoons ought to be reprinted; I am sure modern children would love them.

'Uncle Dick' established a nationwide club called the Wilfredian League of Gugnuncs ('gug' and 'nunc' were among Wilfred's interjections) with Wilfred as President. Members wore blue and silver badges and were issued with a book of rules, containing also the Gugnuncs' song and 'secret' signs and passwords. Each morning on my way to St John's School I passed in Jesus Lane a small girl of about my own age, who with great earnestness exchanged with me both signs and passwords.

****

The biggest hiatus in my education was that I was never encouraged, or for that matter allowed, to learn to play a musical instrument. My father held the firm opinion that musicians were often seduced into bad habits such as playing on pub pianos. My mother was a good pianist, which ought to have reassured him – she never touched alcohol – and my Uncle Humphrey as a professional pianist would gladly have taught me; but it was not to be. It remains one of my greatest regrets that I have never been able to play a musical instrument, for music is one of the great loves of my life.

Yet in another way my father did encourage me in musical appreciation, for he bought a smart gramophone encased in polished mahogany, and every few weeks ordered a supply of records from a London dealer, which arrived, snugly packed in a wooden box. There was a strongly random element in his choice, which might range from the hymn, *Eternal Father, strong to save* (which I was convinced was *Internal Father, strong to save*), to a rendering by the contralto Dame Clara Butt (was there ever another voice as wide-ranging as hers?) of *Land of Hope and Glory* and *Rule Britannia*, recorded in Hyde Park on Empire Day, 1927. In contrast there were 'Here in my Arms' and 'A Tiny Flat in Soho' from *Lido Lady* by Rodgers and Hammerstein, much military music (my father was especially fond of that), selections from Gilbert and Sullivan, Victorian music-hall songs, and such popular contemporary hits as *Forty-seven Ginger-headed Sailors*,

Tip-toe through the Tulips, Tea for Two and *Bye, bye, Blackbird,* as well as songs and selections from Viennese operettas. Although cranking the handle of the gramophone proved a drawback, I spent many happy and contented hours listening to these records, melodies from which still evoke for me a powerful nostalgia.

****

Most Saturday afternoons I went with a few other boys to the Tivoli Cinema on Chesterton Road where for threepence (old pennies) we could sit in the stalls and feast our eyes on films while we sucked boiled sweets or toffee. Some of the films were excellent, among them *The Patriot* (1928) in which Emil Jannings portrayed the mad Tsar Paul; some were revivals of early comedies with Charlie Chaplin, Buster Keaton or Harold Lloyd; and the programme always included the *Topical Budget,* which brought shots of the latest news items, in which leading politicians and royalty could be seen, moving with astonishing alacrity – probably the only way in which one could have seen Queen Mary in a tearing hurry. But the greatest attraction was a weekly serial, each episode lasting about a quarter of an hour, providing us with Grand Guignol excitement. One of these revolved around the misdeeds of a Chinese criminal, Dr. Sin Fang (portrayed by a now-forgotten actor, H. Agar Lyons). Sin Fang always carried an enormous hypodermic syringe, the size of a fly-spray, filled with strong narcotic, with which he rendered his opponents *hors de combat.* It was, however, less than convincing to see how his potential victims passively held their arms on desktops or tables while the needle was inserted, but we were very young, far from critical, and ready to accept with excitement everything offered to us.

I really loved 'the pictures', as we called them. During one of the summer vacations from St John's, I took myself to the Victoria Cinema on Market Hill. The 1927 film *Señorita* was the 'big picture'; it featured Bebe Daniels as a young girl who, to save the fortunes of her family on their Central American hacienda, disguised herself as a young caballero, and successfully fought a rival family, whose leader was played by William Powell, although she nearly perished in the attempt. This I later learned was almost literally true, for she nearly lost an eye in a fencing sequence, and cracked a rib when she leaped from a balcony. Although only nine years old, I fell so deeply in love with Bebe that I spent every penny of my pocket money on visiting the cinema every afternoon for the remainder of the week; I saw the film some six times. When, two or three years later, I saw Miss Daniels in *Río Rita*, I fell in love with her all over again, but this time, after a lapse of a few days, I became reconciled to the unattainability of my idol. I could hardly have expected that I could rival the handsome John Boles, the film's hero.

****

During the summer of 1929, at the age of ten I became seriously ill, indeed close to death, with appendicitis aggravated by peritonitis. Mass was said for my recovery at the Catholic Church, but so that the Catholics should be unable to claim sole credit in the event of my recovery, the staunchly Protestant Miss Heffer (of the bookshop family), matron of the nursing home where I lay, asked the appropriately named Canon Edward Joseph Church of nearby Christ Church, to say prayers for me. This ecumenical effort seems to have worked, for I made a complete and unexpectedly speedy recovery.

In the meantime my father had decided that my education at St John's School was too narrow, and arranged for my entry into the Cambridge and County High School for Boys, to which I was admitted in Autumn 1929. Its headmaster, an unimaginative stick of a man, Arthur Brinley Mayne, M.A. (Oxon), came from Swansea. He was a member of the Headmasters' Conference, so the County School was technically a public school, but that, and Mayne's pathological devotion to corporal punishment, must have been the only common ground it shared with Rugby, Harrow, Uppingham, Haileybury *et al*.

Mayne, nicknamed 'Tishy' after the famous knockkneed racehorse, who also had a mane, was a badly maladjusted man, all brain and no emotion, a living embodiment of Blake's Zoa, Urizen, symbol of the avenging conscience; he should never have been put in charge of the young. He introduced during his

reign three hundred rules of conduct into the school's programme, despite which, or more likely as a direct result of
which, manners and respect for school property declined.
Tishy's own manners would have made a wart-hog seem gen-
teel, so probably his youthful charges followed his example
rather than his advice. As an instance of Tishy's standards, I recall one December afternoon, after the end-of-term Christmas
concert, a crowd of boys, parents and other visitors were leaving
by the main door. Tishy stepped back and trod heavily on my
toe; turning around he began to apologise, but when he realised
it was only *my* toe that he had flattened, he dealt me a great resounding smack of the ear instead.

The stories of Tishy's brutality (the word is not an exaggera-
tion), are legion – I once saw him break two thick canes across
the flinching buttocks of an undersized boy who had done
badly in his end-of-term examinations – but they are best left to
more expert psychological investigators than I. Yet his widespread and it must be added proficient use of the cane, adminis-
tered to punish poor work in addition to what may be considered more properly deserving offences, instilled in many of
the boys in the throes of puberty, an actual enjoyment of beat-
ings, both active and passive, which could, and perhaps in some
cases did, last into maturity.

Some even took pride in their weals and showed them off in
the changing room or lavatories for others to gloat over. This
embarrassed me, but others became dedicated voyeurs; I feel
sure it helped to tip certain boys into pederasty. It was a not un-
common experience for boys of thirteen or fourteen upwards to
be attracted to younger really sexless boys, whose smooth com-
plexions, unhirsute bodies and sometimes almost feminine pret-
tiness, made them the nearest approach to girls that those newly
aware of dawning sexual feelings in a segregated school could
hope to find. And if these little boys bared their behinds to display the marks of a beating, the pederastic urge must have been
almost insupportable; it was usually expressed in an adoring
friendship that dared not allow itself to spill over into physical
sex. Many boys must have been puzzled, perhaps even fright-
ened by their own feelings. Most outgrew them; but how much
better is a modern co-educational school, in which girls are fel-
low-pupils, not a mystery, or a mere distant prospect.

Tishy's staff were a mixed lot. After Tishy himself, its most re-pellent member was 'Bobby' Pask from Yorkshire, the natal county it will be recalled of Wackford Squeers of Dotheboys Hall, Greta Bridge. Pask taught mathematics and physics, em-ploying the bullying humour and heavily sarcastic manner of an old-fashioned sergeant-major. If he perceived any sign of weak-ness in a boy, he would seize upon it and use it to belabour him, to hold him up to the ridicule of his classmates; and there were always plenty of sycophants to roar with simulated laughter at his crude sallies. Not only crude, but repetitive: each Monday we had to recite a geometry theorem, or some other boring mat-ter we had been set to learn at home during the weekend. Bobby's patter was always the same:

'Smith, stand on your hind legs' (chorus of sycophantic laughter). '*Ab initio.*' Poor Smith, whose memory was perhaps indifferent and further impaired by nervousness, would shift about on his feet, trying to recall his task, while Bobby sneered at him, drawing attention to his agitated demeanour. Needless to say, Smith made a complete hash of his repetition. Bobby would then assume a black scowl as he barked, 'Sit. Nought. One hour', sentencing his crestfallen victim to an hour's incar-ceration after school.

Most disgusting of all was Pask's treatment of an unfortunate prefect who suffered from a bad stutter. From time to time he would deliver a message from Tishy to Pask. He had difficulty in enunciating the message, and stood, short of breath, red of countenance and working his mouth into contortions so as to get started, while Pask frowned and irritably and repeatedly urged him to 'spit it out', thus making his second state worse than his first. After more of this browbeating, Pask would make him write it out, while he surveyed the poor fellow in triumph.

It was my misfortune to be in the charge of this dull-minded, walrus-moustached elderly pantaloon during the most traumatic year of my young life, during which the onset of puberty took possession of me like a tornado, leaving me with little spare energy. Under the circumstances I did not deserve Pask's comment on my report at the end of the 1932 Easter Term: 'It is clear that he is thoroughly lazy'. Nor did I deserve, on the same report, the laconic comment of W.J. Lowey, the dull games master: 'Rather lethargic.' At the time it seemed to me that every teacher who instructed me during that year, 1931-2, was set on making my life as difficult as possible.

Moreover, none of them made any allowance for originality. A master who took us for English told us to write for homework an essay on what we considered to be the most important invention of the twentieth century. With one exception the whole class wrote about wireless, as it was then known. I was the exception: with memories of Fritz Lang's film *Metropolis*, which my parents had taken me to see when I was seven, I wrote about robots. Needless to say this brought forth sneers from our usher, who awarded me no marks, and scribbled over my essay in red ink: 'What is the use of them?' Well, if he had lived until the present day, he would be aware that space-exploration, much surgical work, the manufacture of motor-cars, refrigerators and many other useful artefacts, and much else, rely upon robot-operation. Perhaps they are not the century's most significant invention but he ought not to have dismissed my essay with such arrogance: the essay after all was about what *I* considered to be the most important invention. The same pedant scolded me also for referring to a badly-used character in a novel as a 'poor old Jew'. 'He was not poor,' he insisted; 'he had plenty of money'. His Nonconformist soul (he was a Methodist lay-preacher) was unable to visualize spiritual poverty, poverty of mind, or poverty in a dozen other ways; poverty to him would never indicate more than poverty in currency of the realm.

In contrast, one or two men represented a better kind of schoolmaster: dedicated men who would have preferred a more liberal and imaginative kind of education than Tishy's. One of them was my first form-master, Frederick Taylor, a deeply religious man who thereby earned the affectionate sobriquet, 'Holy Joe'. He supervised most subjects in Form I, which consisted of ten- and eleven-year-olds. Although a firm disciplinarian, he was at the same time a kindly man who would go out of his way to explain every detail and every nuance of any subject to his charges. It was due to Holy Joe that during my first year at the County School, I blossomed as a scholar as at no other time during my schooldays, and came top or close to the top of the form in almost every subject. Alas! Holy Joe retired at the end of my first school year.

The art master Harry Brown (nicknamed 'Noddy' because of his slightly shaking head) I found a good-tempered and kindly old fellow, and I did well under his guidance, despite his discouraging remarks when, while still his pupil, I attended evening classes in oil painting under John Hookham (later Ronald Searle's instructor) at the local School of Arts. But Tishy, as one might expect, rated the arts as the very lowest of human attainments, so my success under Noddy did little to forward my school career.

The masters took turns 'on duty', when they presided over detention classes, dealt with various problems, and kept an eye on general behaviour. Noddy took his duties seriously, keeping his eye especially on secretive little groups in chequered shadows under the lime trees surrounding the school field, where covert sexual acts sometimes occurred during warm weather. Other masters did not allow these to bother them, or were too embarrassed to notice; not so Noddy, whose presence always manifested itself to break up such activities. He must have watched the goings-on through binoculars from the staff common-room.

Noddy and his wife, both talented painters and designers, lived graciously and comfortably in a pretty architect-designed house, complete with a studio fitted with a big northern light, and with a dovecote and fantail pigeons in the garden. Here Tishy and his wife came to dinner one evening, and as they were seated at the dining table, Mrs Brown brought in a fine poached salmon. 'Now, Headmaster', said Noddy, 'May I help you to some salmon?' A ghastly grin spread over Tishy's features as he said, 'Fish poisons me!' Noddy might have noticed, had he been more observant, that Tishy never ate fishcakes at school dinner, but was served instead with lamb chops. But perhaps after all poison for Tishy was not such a bad idea.

Boys up to the age of thirteen, by which time their voices had begun to darken, were instructed in singing by a visiting master, the urbane and well-dressed F.E.E. Harvey. An excellent teacher, he helped to fill many gaps in my musical appreciation by introducing me to the rudiments of rhythm, harmony and composition. He coached us in choral singing for performance on speech day; during the two years when I took part in this he made us sing some splendid works which I still love: Handel's *Let the Bright Seraphim*, 'I attempt from love's sickness' from Purcell's *Indian Queen*, and 'Solveig's Song' from Grieg's *Peer Gynt*. Harvey accompanied us on the piano, with his back to the audience, silently mouthing the words to us like a human auto-cue.

At various times during my career at the County School, I was taught French by Gilbert Mantell, in some ways an endearing character, with a robust sense of humour, fragmented at times by outbursts of unpredictable bad temper. He may not have been the best of instructors, but in those days French was in any case taught with a complete lack of imagination, and with horrid phonetics, which one had to unlearn when one got on to writing the language properly, not as now, as a conversational living language. Mantell endeavoured to make the subject a bit more appealing, and from time to time took us through pages from French newspapers. His efforts were nevertheless undermined by a tendency to exaggerate and tell us tall stories, even downright lies. When we complained that it was difficult to understand what French people were saying because they spoke so fast, he flatly denied the implication saying that in fact they spoke much more slowly than the English, which was demonstrably untrue. His most valuable contribution to our education was to encourage the proper study of philately, as opposed to the mere accumulation of postage stamps. He had a fine collection and became a leading authority, especially in the early stamps of this country. He started a school stamp club and appointed me as its secretary: it was quite successful, and he even held a few auctions of boys' duplicates, but strictly enjoined us to keep quiet about them, since he feared Tishy might not approve. Mantell played the violin and sang, but stretched his untrained baritone voice beyond its capabilities; his rendering at a school concert of the notoriously difficult 'Toreador's Song' from *Carmen* became particularly painful.

He was a leading light in the school's Officers' Training Corps, which boys were expected to join when they were old enough, although we could join the Boy Scouts as an alternative. For a year or two I chose the alternative, and even took part in the Troop's summer camp in 1931 at Borth, near Aberystwyth, an experience I did not relish at the time, although in retrospect it seems to have been pleasant enough. The scoutmaster, Horace Avron Cartledge, was a genial man who taught French to boys in junior forms; to me his chief attraction was a nervous tic which enabled him to move his ears back and forth, an attainment I tried with ill success to emulate.

The O.T.C. lacked recruits, due probably to the influence of T.P.R. Layng, a master who never neglected an opportunity to inculcate socialist and pacifist views and ideas into the minds of his pupils. When a senior officer made his annual visit to inspect the Corps, Layng would comment, 'The professional murderer has come to inspect the amateur murderers', a declaration that in itself must have been enough to deter many boys from enlisting. Be that as it may, Tishy became seriously worried about the paucity of recruits, and called an assembly in the school hall of those old enough to volunteer, but who so far had neglected to do so. He made what for him was an impassioned appeal, claiming that it was the Territorial Army that saved England from disaster in 1914, a simplistic and highly questionable claim that other branches of the services would have treated with derision. Tishy, as was his wont on such occasions, fixed his saurian eye on one unfortunate boy throughout his address, with the result that the lad, reduced to an extreme of nervousness, threw up on the floor.

Tishy's appeal had little effect, for it produced few, if any, new recruits. I firmly set my face against the idea. We had heard in the meantime, and soon it was confirmed, that Tishy had himself not served in any of the armed services in the 1914-18 War. On the other hand, he was now continuing the tradition of many older men during that War, urging the young to join up and risk their lives, while they stayed at home and felt patriotic.

Following the ghastly period of subjection to Bobby Pask's vilification, I began to achieve some ascendancy in some other subjects such as history, English and scripture, the master in charge of which was Leonard Hollingworth, himself a minor writer of detective fiction. Hollingworth's lessons were more appealing to me than those of any master since the retirement of Holy Joe. Nicknamed 'Snap' from his clipped manner of speech, he taught me during my fourteenth year. So good was his method that I came top of the form in all three of his subjects, both in examinations and in classwork. To recalcitrant pupils, Snap would say: 'I do my best to make these lessons interesting; if you choose to ignore what I am trying to impart to you, you are free to do so, but keep quiet so that others may enjoy them.' Needless to say he received full attention thereafter.

Another important matter was that Snap went out of his way to reassure us about our status. We were in form 4C when he first taught us, and Tishy and his close minions repeatedly reminded us that we were inferior to boys in the A and B streams. Not so Snap: he told us that Winston Churchill, for whom he had what was then an unfashionable admiration, left school when he was in form 4C at Harrow, yet still went on to become a great statesman and a noted historian. Moreover he made a point of telling us that boys from C forms were likely to develop with greater originality in later life than the usually more conventional boys from A forms: especially they made excellent businessmen. Without doubt he was right in this: many of my classmates had success in commerce, and some amassed considerable fortunes – from an earlier generation, Sir David Robinson was a prime example – while many of the A and B people ended as disgruntled parsons and disagreeable schoolmasters.

During my year in 4C I managed a narrow escape from an early death. A boy from a higher form, considerably senior to, and much more powerful than, myself, seemed for some unexplained reason to have taken a dislike to me, and one afternoon in the cloakroom he pinioned me from behind, took each end of my scarf in his hands, and attempted to strangle me. I am not sure how close to success he came, but I did lose consciousness. He was stopped by the opportune appearance in the doorway of Harry Hatton, the gardener, who apparently shouted at my attacker that he ought to have his nose punched. I became hysterical during the ensuing night, and my father prised out of me the details of what had happened. The next morning he went to see Tishy, fully determined on having a first-class row. This proved unnecessary, for Tishy took the matter seriously enough, to the extent that my adversary bothered me no more.

What neither he nor anybody else could rectify, however, was the delayed effect of the attack, for not long afterwards I was laid low by a highly unpleasant neurosis, the main symptom of which was an inability to clear my mind of the thought of death and of my own eventual and inescapable demise. It is difficult to describe the complete terror, with its complicated manifestations, that dominated me for two or three months. In vain my father, having experienced a similar condition as a young man, tried to reassure me by telling me that death was nothing to fear, that it was as natural to die as to be born. At times I would dash from the house, and run and run, panic-stricken and without aim, until I was physically exhausted. At other times I would sit, unable to relieve my mind by reading, painting or drawing, unable to think of anything but the spectre dominating my soul. To go near to a churchyard or a cemetery, or to see a passing funeral cortège, was to call up all the fiends of Hell, for I became terrified of premature burial (on which subject I had recently read Edgar Allan Poe).

My condition was further exacerbated by the death of Grandad Arnold at the early age of sixty-six, though in fact he looked much older than that. His originally robust constitution – in his heyday he could almost have fought a lion – had been weakened by heart disease, brought on by the strain of overwork. His funeral, the first I had ever attended, took place on a wet, melancholy day, with a requiem mass at the Catholic Church. At the interment at the Borough Cemetery my mother broke down completely: I have never seen anybody weep so bitterly. There was no lightening of the soul on this dreary day and my depression passed beyond support.

Soon afterwards, Dr. Lloyd Jones was called in to examine me, and wisely prescribed complete rest, with a course of sedative. In time the attack burned itself out, but it did recur from time to time until, and even after, I reached adulthood. A nightmarish visitation came when I was forty, but I was better able to deal with it then, than when I was fourteen.

****

During my last eighteen months at school, my greatest friend was W. R. Jarman, an unusually gifted pianist and organist, the son of a farmer at Whaddon, near Royston in Hertfordshire. During his earliest days at the County School he had fallen foul of one of the more disagreeable masters, Newdigate ('Two, four, six, eight') Poyntz, and played truant for many weeks. It is hardly necessary to add that this led to a first-class scandal, but Jarman, who had plenty of character, maintained his dignity, and by the time we became friends, was respected by the staff, who had come to realise that in argument and repartee he proved no mean opponent.

Jarman used to tell me of piano sonatas he wanted to compose, I used to show him my drawings, and we developed a deep mutual respect. Alas! after I left school, and after a brief correspondence, we lost touch, and when I next heard of him, it was that he had died in the Singapore debâcle in 1941. I wonder how many more such creative spirits perished in that War. And I wonder if he ever composed those sonatas, and if he did, what became of them.

Like many youngsters I felt inclined to flit from subject to subject, but I do not see any particular harm in that, for the very diversity of these interests laid a wide, if not very deep, foundation of knowledge and appreciation. Even if I did not delve very deeply, my many fleeting interests provided points of departure for later, more detailed and concentrated study. When I was fourteen, I began to collect Roman coins. A local antique dealer in Bridge Street, F. R. Whitaker, kept a most interesting shop which contained all manner of antiques and curiosities, among which were one or two numismatic cabinets containing bronze coins of Claudius, Vespasian, Hadrian and others, priced at sixpence (2.5p) apiece. I bought one of these each week out of my one shilling (5p) a week pocket money.

Whitaker was an imposing, at times forbidding character. Some claimed that he was an illegitimate son of King Edward VII. I do not know, but it is a fact that his manner was regal, his appearance aristocratic: prominent features, grey hair brushed up into a great coil, a moustache of comparable proportions and long, elegant hands, on one of which he wore a large ruby ring. One never asked him the price of anything – to do so was a *faux pas*. It had to be volunteered by him as an afterthought, when he had finished discoursing upon the artistic or historical significance of the object. But he was not unhelpful; one day after I had bought a coin, he turned to an elderly gentleman who was looking through his cabinets, and said: 'Professor Cook, I wonder if you would tell my young friend something about the coin he has just bought.' The Professor eyed me benevolently, took up the coin and informed me that it was a Greek coin, minted at Alexandria, and had a figure of Nike on its reverse. He then picked up another coin and handed it to me saying, 'Please take this one, too, as a present from me.' I have seldom encountered luck like that. I still have both coins, and I discovered later that the Professor was the eminent classic and archaeologist, Arthur Bernard Cook (1868-1952).

Because of my various interests, I became a frequent visitor to the Fitzwilliam Museum. In the coin room, Harold Shrubbs, the chief numismatic assistant, was very kind and tremendously patient with my pertinacious questions, and showed me anything I asked to see, from Syracusan dekadrachms to silver pennies of Saxon kings. A passing interest in Egyptology and hieroglyphics led to Eric Clark, an assistant in that department, giving me access to his reference books whenever I could find time after school hours to look at them. William Ryder, the chief assistant, and to me a very grand personage indeed, was kindness personified in dozens of different ways.

Cousins was always there, tirelessly arousing and nursing my interest in subject after subject, whether it was to draw my attention to a portrait by Fantin-Latour, to particularly choice specimens of English or Netherlandish horae, to books printed by William Morris at the Kelmscott Press, or to a Madonna and Child painted by Andrea Vanni. He would point out that it was not necessary for fine works of art to be old, and would tell me what books – fiction, text books, what you will – to read, always guiding me into new avenues of appreciation. Strange, it may be thought, that a man with little formal education should possess such a wide cultural background (he was also a self-taught, yet accomplished pianist), and should be able to arouse such enthusiasm in a young schoolboy. But strange or not, this was the reality of Albert Cousins, whom I learned to respect and love.

During my fifteenth year I decided to try my hand at illuminating, something better than had been possible from my enthusiastic, but rather clumsy juvenile hands at St John's. Of necessity the results were still primitive: they included the text of *Matthew* Chapter 27, with a miniature of the Crucifixion included. Although I no longer possess this I do still have a couple of longer illuminated MSS which I made a year or perhaps eighteen months later: one of the Anglo-Catholic Eucharist, the other embodying a little of the Lister and Arnold family histories. They are crude enough in all conscience, and there are few people to whom I would be prepared to show them, but they do afford a slight indication of what I would accomplish in the way of miniature painting during the following decades. For it was not long before I began to realise that calligraphy and manuscript decoration were not for me, and that the miniature was my ideal medium.

From the beginning I showed each of my efforts to Cousins for comment and criticism, which he always gave unstintingly and conscientiously. Sparing me nothing, he indicated my many faults of technique, composition and conception. I am sure he always appreciated what I hoped to achieve, and although, in my own interest, he offered a great deal of criticism, he also showed enthusiasm and encouragement, and his criticism was imparted with such kindness and respect that it constituted in itself an incitement to continue and improve. He generously imparted to me receipts for the mixing of colours, for the preparation of gold size, albumen and vellum, that he had with pains and experiment acquired over the years; my technique in miniature painting owes more to him than I could ever express.

****

My father's early encouragement, the influence of good reading at St John's School and in Hollingworth's classes at the County School, to which may be added the lure of the beauty of illuminated manuscripts, set me at an early age on the path of book collecting. By the time I left school I had a modest little collection, mostly finely printed modern books, in a bookcase of my own. This interest inevitably brought me while I was still at school to that bibliophilic Mecca, David's bookstall on Market Hill.

Gustave David, a cosmopolitan of mixed Jewish and French

descent, used to sit by his stall on an old wooden box dressed in a shabby overcoat, Homburg hat and spats, as he is depicted in a well-known drawing by William Nicholson. While he sat there and chain-smoked and read an endless succession of French novels, potential customers browsed among his ever-changing stock, finding perhaps a 17th century Bible for five shillings (25p), a Thomas Hardy first edition for a shilling, or an incunabulum 'with all faults' for under a pound. David could be irascible. When I was about fourteen I saw a book on the Victorian theatre which I coveted; I asked if I might see it, but as soon as I saw the price marked inside, seven shillings and sixpence (37.5p), I realised that it was far beyond my meagre pocket-money. Apologetically and regretfully I handed it back to him, and he snatched it out of my hand and flung it back on top of the other books with a deep growl of disapproval. Yet I must not complain, for I later acquired many real bargains from him and from his successor, his son Hubert.

Art and literature were not my only schoolboy interests. I was also passionately absorbed in astronomy. I had (still have) an old mariner's telescope made by S. and S. Lee of Leamington, which had belonged to Grandad Lister, and I used it to gaze at the lunar mountains, and as for sidereal study it demonstrated that there were endless myriads of stars scattered over the empyrean like pollen. It gave me, too, some satisfaction to feel that I had one piece of optical equipment to further my interest, and to this a little later, when pocket money would allow, I added a planisphere of the pattern still marketed by Philips, the cartographic publishers. I also equipped myself with a number of books, bought with a handsome tip from Granny Lister, among them *Popular Astronomy* (first published 1880) by Camille Flammarion. The Solar Physics Observatory on Madingley Road was open on certain afternoons to members of the University and their friends. Undaunted by this declared restriction, I presented myself there several times, asking if I might be shown around. As in the case of the Fitzwilliam staff, it says much for the kindness and patience of those in charge that they put their work aside to explain in considerable detail what was going on.

For my Christmas gift in 1932, my parents presented me with a wonderful box of educational scientific equipment called

'Construments', from which a boy could construct working microscopes, various types of camera, and other instruments. It was a wonderful idea and it is puzzling that it quickly disappeared from the market. It occurred to me that with some of this equipment, used in conjunction with my grandfather's telescope, I might be able to construct an astronomical camera. I told one of the men at the Observatory about this; he said it was a good idea, but that the image on the photographic plate would be only about one-eighth of an inch in diameter, thereby severely limiting its usefulness. I did in fact construct the camera, and of course he was right – it was impractical. But it gave me at least a little insight into the simplest principles of astronomical photography.

Soon after this my ambitions outran my commonsense, when I tried to embrace all kinds of scientific subjects: zoology, physics, chemistry, even meteorology. I requisitioned a wooden shed that stood in our garden, dubbed it 'The Cam Observatory', and inserted an advertisement in a boy's magazine, inviting correspondence. Strangely enough, it caught the attention of one or two more mature enthusiasts, professional scientists, who wrote suggesting an exchange of data. The Arnold family heard of this, and for a time my life was made unbearable by endless badinage. True, there were one or two exceptions, among them Uncle Humphrey Lant who kindly congratulated me on the way in which I had worded the advertisement; but despite this, my scientific interests were then and there abandoned. In fairness, I must say that it is doubtful if I should have been able to continue them for long, if only because of my mathematical insufficiency. Nevertheless I should have appreciated a little encouragement.

Yet I was lucky to have been born and brought up in Cambridge. With the exception of Oxford, its ambience differs from that of any other English town. If one is at all sensitive to culture, one is exposed in Cambridge to all kinds of beneficial influence: recently I was discussing this with an old friend who had been one of my contemporaries at the County School, and is now a successful lawyer, until recently holding a post as a legal adviser to the Government. We agreed that if our youth had been spent elsewhere, the story of our lives, and of what success we have enjoyed, would probably have been different in the first and diminished in the second.

****

On my fifteenth birthday, 28 March 1934, I left school. My father had descried that I should never prosper under Tishy's regime, and despite my spectacular improvement under one or two masters like Leonard Hollingworth this did seem to be the case. So my schooldays ended, and on 29 March, the very next day, I was bound apprentice to the family firm.

The first thing I did after walking out of the school gates and depositing my school cap in the nearest refuse basket, was to walk with Jarman into the centre of Cambridge, and visit Heffer's bookshop in Petty Cury, where I bought a copy of George Bernard Shaw's *Adventures of the Black Girl in her Search for God* (1932), illustrated with John Farleigh's splendid wood-engravings. I suppose this symbolised the breaking of my scholastic chains, for the book, in which Shaw cocked a snook at nonsensical aspects of orthodox theology, was enjoying a certain notoriety. I, too, could now at long last cock a snook at Tishy Mayne, his school and his methods, and though I was to be bound apprentice I felt sweetly at liberty.

Five
Prentice Years

*

The engineering firm in which I was apprenticed had existed since 1890, when it was founded by my grandfather, George Lister, and two partners, the blacksmiths Charles Flatters and Harry Branch. At first the workshop was little more than a shed at the bottom of my grandfather's garden, but within a few years they acquired more land and built on it a large workshop of brick and tiles. By the year of my birth Flatters and Branch had been bought out by my grandfather, who soon afterwards took his sons, my father and my Uncle Alf, into partnership.

When I was a child the workshop had grown apace, indeed had become several workshops. The machine shop, with its lathes, radial drills, milling, planing and shaping machines, was the biggest. In a corner of this, a partition enclosed a small area containing a desk, a stool and pigeon-holes. This Grandad used as a works office and as a store; it was connected to the main office at the front of the premises by a wall-telephone. Access from the machine shop to the blacksmiths' shop was through a small open doorway. The engine room, in a corner of the blacksmiths' shop, housed the old National gas engine which wheezed, coughed and banged through the day. The blacksmiths' shop, like the machine shop, had tall windows along its front elevation, under which wooden benches had been fitted with a row of heavy vices. In front of each of the four brick forges stood an anvil on its support – a section of a large tree-trunk. Rows of set hammers, tongs, punches, wrenches and other hand tools hung on wall-racks between the forges, and other items of blacksmithing equipment lay around on the floor, including mandrels for shaping rings, heavy swage blocks with grooves and perforations for shaping red-hot bars, and a plane plate for marking out work. The only machines were a couple of drilling machines, a power-driven punch and shear for severing bars and punching holes, and a rotary fan for blowing up the hearths. In earlier days air for this had been supplied from a great hand-bellows which still stood in one corner, over the foreman's desk.

In line with this building stood a more recent one, also built of brick and tile. My grandfather originally intended it to be a foundry but, at the time of which I am writing, it was actually used for automobile work. My Uncle Alf had returned from service as a sapper during the Great War, fired with enthusiasm for automobile engineering and determined to develop it in the business. For this a couple of inspection pits were dug in the floor. While they were being excavated, some ancient fragments of human skeletons were unearthed. They must have been there for centuries, and may well have belonged to occupants of the huge Augustinian Priory which once covered the area. The story goes that the bones were mixed with the concrete which lined the pits; if this is true these unfortunates will have some difficulty when the Last Trump heralds the general Resurrection.

My uncle's automobile work was not the firm's first experience of these machines. In the 1890s a well-to-do parson, the Rev. G. B. Finch, had been one of the first, if not the very first, Cambridge resident to own a motor-car, serviced by my grandfather. Automobile engineering disappeared from the business almost completely after my uncle's early death in 1929, to be revived for a few years in a different form in the 1950s when, under the supervision of my brother Brian, we made sports/racing motor-cars which enjoyed success on various racing circuits in England and abroad.

At right angles to this workshop stood another covered area between what was once Branch's home and the house of our general foreman. It was terminated at the road – Abbey Road – and was closed by a fine pair of wrought iron gates, which, when the business was in 1967 moved to a new site, I presented in memory of my grandfather to Burwell parish church in Cambridgeshire, where they still stand. In this area stood steam traction-engines brought in for repair and overhaul, which remained a vitally important part of our business until 1939. The general office, built in about 1900 on the road frontage, was divided into two rooms. The outer room accommodated a general clerk and her assistant; the inner one was my grandfather's and later my father's private office. Such was the extent of its premises near to the end of the first half-century of the firm's existence, and during the period of my apprenticeship.

Of the men who worked there, two became especially important to me, and taught me much of what I know about the crafts practised by the firm. The more impressive was Samuel Albert Mason, the firm's chief blacksmith and general foreman, a giant of a man who in his heyday weighed seventeen stone or more. He worked for three generations of the Lister family, and retired in 1949 after spending fifty years with us. He was one of the most skilled of the many blacksmiths it has been my privilege to know. Today his work, anonymous in most cases, may be seen on many buildings throughout the country. Sometimes it is functional, sometimes it is decorated with a few scrolls; at others it proliferates into masks, leaves and flowers – madonna lilies, roses, clematis – so delicately wrought that if they were painted in natural colours, it would, without touching them, be difficult to be sure that they were not the real thing.

I found it stimulating to see Sam at work, his huge hands with their thick but sensitive fingers lovingly hammering a bar of red hot iron into graceful scrolls which often terminated in decorations, teased and wreathed from the raw bar in which they had been hidden. From time to time he would hold his forging up and compare it with the drawing or offer it up to its template. When satisfied, he plunged it into the water trough before flinging it on the floor where it would remain until the time came to fit it into its final position. Thus, out of a heap of forged components, Sam would assemble an elegant balcony rail, balustrade, gate, screen, lantern, weather vane or one of a hundred other works, forge-welding them together (electric- and gas-welding were eschewed), riveting or banding them into place, until the whole work seemed to flow, almost pulsate, like water beneath fountains.

It is not surprising that I, always drawn to the arts, should have preferred this to operating machines such as centre-lathes, milling machines and radial drills, to which trade I was nominally apprenticed, and from which I tried to escape, whenever an opportunity presented itself, into the blacksmiths' shop and the kindly and inspiring tutelage of Sam Mason. Indeed blacksmithery beckoned me with growing intensity, and so did its sister trade of locksmithery, which incidentally is not necessarily connected with locks and keys, neither of which I ever touched, but to decorative work made in locksmith's technique: shaped cold by means of files, chisels and drills. I liked the jewelled brilliance that could in this way be realised, but it must be admitted that blacksmithery, in which the iron is shaped by hammers, stamps and punches on an anvil, at red or white heat, has an intensity, an urgency, a sense of flowing progression without parallel in any other form of metalwork.

Decorative ironwork became even more attractive to me when I began to realise that much of the work on which I was engaged would be installed in such historic settings as college chapels, in Carmelite convents throughout Britain (ever since my grandfather's day we had made their choir and communion grilles), in grand houses in town and country, in churches, cathedrals and castles. There was something special about making candlesticks for lighting the choir in King's College Chapel, wrought iron doors filled with glass for a house in London's Park Lane, a gate and screen to enclose an area in Selwyn College, chancel gates for a famous church in the City of London, or a weathervane for a Scottish castle. But, when war broke out in 1939, a few months after the end of my apprenticeship, all of this had to be put aside and replaced by work which was thought (no doubt rightly at the time) of greater importance than our artistic heritage.

The man under whom I learned my trade as a machine-operator and fitter, was a vastly different personality from Sam: foreman of the machine shop, Ernest William Fox, son of a noted local detective. By the time I became an apprentice in 1934, he was the sole remaining centre-lathe turner who had learned his trade direct from my grandfather; he was therefore a magician with a lathe, and never defeated by a machining problem, however insoluble it may have appeared. He taught me much of what I know about that aspect of the firm's work, though I am sure that my lack of real interest must have made me a disappointing pupil.

I never found life dull with Ernie around, though it must be admitted that his sardonic, indeed often somewhat cruel sense of humour did not make him generally endearing. Nobody found it funny to be on the receiving end of an electric shock from a magneto wired to one's vice. Nor, if one was behindhand with a job, to find a great lump of moss laid on it. And especially, it was a painful experience to arise from a lavatory seat to which spots of belt grip had been applied. All of these practical jokes and many more, could be laid at Ernie's door, to say nothing of his jeering personal comments about the domestic lives of some of the men.

Yet Ernie's complex, almost baroque, personality could also be sensitive, even romantic at times, and he could be capable of great kindness. One of his greatest pleasures was derived from his allotment, where he grew some of the finest carnations I have ever seen: picotees, bizarres, flakes, with enormous flowers that still retained the now rare clove scent. When, as a young boy, I was recovering from a serious illness, Ernie sent me at the nursing home a huge bouquet of these flowers, which must have denuded his allotment; I shall for ever associate their Malmaison piquancy with the light buoyancy of convalescence.

****

My first job as an apprentice was as mate to one of our fitters, Bill Rouse, when he installed air-conditioning in the bottling store at the nearby Star Brewery. This installation meant that several men would be dismissed as redundant, and one morning while we were at work they were given their notices. What a bacchanalian scene ensued! Those under notice moved as if they were part of a self-propelled amorphous mass, rolled a barrel into the centre of the store, stood it on its end and knocked in the upper end with a hammer. They spent the remainder of the morning ladling its contents down their gullets. It amazed, it still amazes me, to see how much those men could drink and still remain upright, if nevertheless in a state of unstable equilibrium. Within half an hour they were drunk, yet three hours later they still stood around the barrel, steadying themselves by its rim, drinking like fishes, and standing in the spilled beer that now lay in huge puddles on the floor.

I worked long hours as an apprentice. I began each day at 6.30 a.m., with a break from 8.30 to 9 a.m. for breakfast; the second session continued from 9 a.m. to 1 p.m., followed by a luncheon break from 1 p.m. to 2 p.m.; the third session lasted from 2 p.m. to 5 p.m. On Saturday, a half-holiday, I knocked off at 12.30 p.m. For a few months, until I got used to the hours, I seemed perpetually dead tired. Later, I came to enjoy the early start, especially on crisp mornings in spring and autumn – at any rate, I acquired an appetite which might have been envied by Gargantua; never again since those years have I been able to consume such huge breakfasts.

My father by this time had complete control of the firm, which he had taken over on the death of my grandfather in January 1930. From the moment he took over, he set about modernising it. Time-sheets were introduced to replace the grubby slates hitherto used; stores for the first time were put under lock and key, in charge of a storekeeper; he installed electric welding, then quite a rare phenomenon; in the office he introduced modern accounting practices. Such improvements led to an enormous increase in business efficiency, and profits began to climb.

Like my grandfather, my father continued to insist that our craftsmanship must be of the best, for he rightly realised that such consistency was one of the firm's greatest assets. He never tired of claiming that success in business was easy if three basic rules were observed: high quality of workmanship, a fair price, and reliable delivery forecast. It was this insistence, coupled with modernisation, that brought him prosperity undreamed of by his father and grandfather.

He drummed his ideas into me during meal after meal, evening after evening. Every aspect of the crafts we practised was explained, every tool and machine I was likely to encounter was analysed, its capabilities and limitations defined. When he decided to invest in some new item of equipment he would hand me a textbook and ask me to read the relevant passages aloud to him, so that we each ingested at least the theory of its working and application. Similarly, he rehearsed business practices over and over again. I doubt if any young man ever received more detailed and concentrated instruction than I received from my father. He took me with him to interview customers, to buy machinery; he called me into his office when he was giving jobs their final invoice prices (no job, however small, was ever invoiced without his approval), so that I should be aware of how much each was worth; I sat with him when he received suppliers' representatives. Apart from this I spent my working hours in the workshops, where I gleaned details of every practical facet of our trade, and at the same time ripened my own mastery of its skills. I must confess that at the time I found many of these discussions bothersome, for one's 'teens are not the best period for coping with business routine. But I felt thankful for them later, when I had the task of managing a great part of the business.

Horace Lister was a strong character, at times overbearing and autocratic, but only a man of such determination could have weathered the 1931 crisis with the full complement of his staff working overtime. He could be thoughtful, too, and if the need arose could be kind and understanding. Yet he had the defects of his good points, and when his irritable fibre was uppermost could be incredibly perverse. I quarrelled with him more often than I can recall; but although afterwards he might be unapproachable for days ultimately he always eagerly buried the hatchet and started afresh.

I am sure that I, and others, made insufficient allowance for the burden of responsibilities he shouldered alone during the years following his father's death. These included an undertaking to buy out, within two years, his father's share in the firm; this in addition to striving to update it, and travelling all over the eastern counties to drum up trade. So, if at times he lost patience with my adolescent posturings and outpourings, he was to be forgiven. And when after one contretemps, he shouted, 'My God! I hope if ever you have a son, he will be as irritating a bugger as you!', I remember it with understanding.

One evening we had a stand-up row in the hall of our house after which I stalked away and slammed the front door with every bit of force and weight I could summon. When I returned about four hours later, my mother emerged from the drawing room and said, with an understanding grin, 'If I were you I should go up to bed before your father sees you. When you slammed the door a plate fell off the panelling and broke on his head!' I needed no further warning, and made myself scarce. On that occasion a week or two passed before things returned to normal.

Waiters and other hotel staff sometimes ran foul of him, though not always because of his fault. A foolish, or inexperienced waiter was standing behind him during luncheon in a Brighton hotel, holding a bowl of new potatoes. Somehow my father had caught his jacket on the arm of his chair, causing its collar to lie back from his shirt. Into this aperture, in a moment of inattention, the wretched waiter tipped the contents of his bowl, as he stepped forward to serve him. My father jumped to his feet and the whole lot fell out of the bottom of his jacket, for all the world like a horse relieving itself. How he managed to keep his hands off that waiter I shall never be able to understand. In a man of such choleric temperament I found it an example of superb self-control. Similarly, on arrival at a Bournemouth hotel, a porter emerged to collect my father's suitcase from the car, and made the ghastly mistake of pressing himself into the same compartment of the revolving doors, pushing the case between Father's legs. The ensuing combination of desperate fighting, frenzied oaths and slow but inexorable progress into the hotel reception hall, looked like an episode in a P.G. Wodehouse novel.

Yet he behaved with considerable dignity, and few would dare to take a liberty. One of the few able to penetrate this wall was Dr. Lloyd Jones, himself a man of strong character. In the late 1930s my father had an infection in one of his ears and called on Lloyd Jones at his consulting rooms for an auricular examination. The doctor asked Father to step into the bay window and inserted his auriscope. 'How very curious,' he remarked, 'I can see King's College Chapel through here!' 'Sarcastic old bugger', said Father when he told us about it; all the same he wore a wry grin on his face.

He was strongly hypochondriac, and if any of us was ill and

medicine had been prescribed, Father always had to drink a dose of it. He loved to visit Lloyd Jones, whose prescriptions he hoarded against possible recurrent attacks. Quite often he took double doses on the assumption that he would, by so doing, recover in half the time. When he was an old man, his doctor (Lloyd Jones had died ere this) sometimes prescribed antibiotics; at such times Father left the courses uncompleted and built up a store of the capsules, a few of which he invariably carried in his waistcoat pocket, and at the least sign of a cold, would pop one into his mouth as a safeguard. This sounds terribly risky, but strangely enough it seems to have done him no harm, for he lived a perfectly healthy life until he died within a month of his eightieth birthday.

One of Father's most attractive traits lay in his fondness for and understanding of young children, in whose fantasies he participated as an equal, relating stories of elves he claimed to have met on woodland walks, embroidering his anecdotes into ever greater elaboration; in a strange way they became more believable as they were developed – perhaps because he seemed to believe them himself. There was, when I was a little boy, a nanitic watchmaker on Chesterton Road, a Mr. T. Westrop. When Father took me with him to collect a watch repair, he told me he was an elf, and I was more than half inclined to believe him. Another manifestation of his affection for children was that each Christmas until 1939, he treated all the children in a local orphanage to a matinée performance of a pantomime at one of the local theatres.

****

Through the years of my apprenticeship I felt progressively more stifled by the Catholic Church. Priests visited me from time to time in efforts to bring me back into the fold. In certain circles of the Arnold family there was excess of inflexibility, indeed bigotry, that left no room for original or independent thought. Conversely it was also true that a few of them had turned their backs on it (one was my mother's brother Tom, incidentally one of my godparents), and its influence was successfully withstood by some of those, my father included, who had married into the family.

Yet I still felt a lacuna in my life, and began to look elsewhere, making the mistake of looking for a variation in what Blake called 'the outward Ceremony'. I turned in my teens to Anglo-Catholicism, and for a few months attended services at St. Giles's, then the main Anglo-Catholic church in Cambridge. The ritual at St Giles's closely resembled that of the Roman Catholic Church, and although I eventually came to the conclusion that it was imitative, for the time being I felt happy, indeed sufficiently enthusiastic to make myself a little altar in my bedroom, with a crucifix flanked by candlesticks, and a series of cloth covers of the colours of the successive ecclesiastical seasons. To one side of this stood a small triptych, with a print of Saint Francis preaching to the birds, which I had bought at Buckfast Abbey during a recent holiday. Only lack of funds prevented me from buying a thurible and a supply of incense. I decided to be confirmed and asked one of the clergy, the eminent historian, the Rev. Charles Smyth, if he would prepare me.

At first all went well, but when I began to ask awkward questions, not from bravado, but because there were things I could not understand, Smyth decided he could not cope, and passed me on to the Vicar. This was the worst thing he could have done, for this parson, the Rev. C.C.H. James, was one of the most snobbish and pompous asses it has been my misfortune to know. He took a high-handed supercilious attitude, told me I was holding a gun at his head, did not bother to answer one of my questions, told me I was ignorant (that I knew; I was struggling for enlightenment), and bundled me out of his vicarage as fast as he could. I packed away my little altar, and next went, as I ought to have done in the first place, to my old friend Sam Senior, who took enormous trouble to clarify my puzzlement, and generally treated me as if I were an intelligent being. His evangelical Church of England precepts contrasted favourably with the Catholicism practised at St. Giles's. But it got me nowhere. My mother, now that I was coming to the point of confirmation, raised strong objections, insisting that if I wanted to be confirmed it must be as a Catholic. My father, who had so far encouraged me, withdrew his support and refused to give me time off from work to attend the confirmation service.

I confided all this to Sam, who suggested he should visit my parents and talk things over with them, but I was so completely embarrassed and upset by the whole business, that I begged him to accept the situation. I felt thoroughly defrauded – my father, after all, had encouraged my independent ideas – with the consequence that I never again attempted to become formally accepted into any church, and looking back, I am not sorry.

In time, during her later years, Mother's opinion of the Catholic Church was much modified. She came to express real dislike of it, not altogether for the reasons that my father was against it, still less for my own reasons, but on ethical grounds, for what she saw as its lack of respect for the individual, for its bigotry, for its manipulative practices which she considered amounted often to religious blackmail, and for its grasping practices in raising funds. No doubt my father's opinions influenced her somewhat, but she was a woman of strongly independent mind, and would in any case have thought things through for herself, whatever his attitude. The final turning point came when Auntie Ruby, her youngest and favourite sister, died at the early age of forty-seven. Ruby was a devout Catholic, had attended mass regularly, had performed all her duties well, but she was not well-off, had little to contribute to church funds, and had nothing to bequeath to them. When the day arrived, her requiem mass was pushed into an unattractive side chapel with pews swivelled round at an angle to accommodate the rather large congregation, giving the occasion a decidedly uninspiring atmosphere. Mother was furious to realise that her sister's requiem had been carried through with such lack of respect, with such little regard for the feelings of her husband, children and family.

Later, when Mother lay seriously ill, she was asked at the hospital to give her religion, to which she answered, 'If I need help, please send for Mr Sam Senior'. And on her deathbed she expressed the wish that her funeral service should be that of the Church of England.

Six
The Arts Beckon

My apprenticeship may have been demanding, but artistic outlets I had to have. I continued to paint, to read about the arts in everything I could lay my hands on, and I continually visited Cousins at the Fitzwilliam Museum to talk and to seek his views and opinions. Although up to that time I had had little contact with the University (in those days town and gown were mutually exclusive), I joined the University Arts Society as a peripheral member, and found most of the lectures held under its aegis well worth attending: Graham Sutherland, John Betjeman and Frank Murphy of Murphy Radio, who talked about his designs for furniture, were among celebrities who addressed us.

Betjeman imparted a characteristic flavour to his talk on architecture, claiming that the most interesting building in Cambridge was not King's College Chapel, Wren's Chapel at Pembroke College, Gibbs's Senate House, or indeed anything of that kind, but the art nouveau shop of the Stetchworth Dairies in Market Street. This was a gross overstatement, but at least it sent some of us round to Market Street to look at the shop with a new eye. And it helped to demonstrate the pleasures of art nouveau, two or three decades before the style was seen in historical perspective, and once again became a fashionable cult.

Just before the outbreak of war, undergraduate members of the University Arts Society organised an exhibition of their work. Mounted in the Round Church Hall, it was largely made up of posturing anti-war stuff – one painting was framed in barbed wire. Greatly daring, I submitted two of my miniatures, which could hardly have been more out of place in such company, and while they were not exactly forbidden entry to the exhibition, they were not hung on the walls with the other works, but placed loosely on a table without labels to indicate what they were and who painted them. Nevertheless word got around that they were my work, and subsequently they were highly praised in a report of the exhibition in the local newspaper, while one or two of the professional artists who visited the exhibition took trouble to congratulate me on them. They included the talented painter and etcher, Marjorie Sherlock, former pupil of Sickert and Malcolm Osborne, who thereafter became a close and encouraging friend, fearless and generous with praise if anybody spoke slightingly of my work.

****

The theatre absorbed much of my spare time during my apprenticeship. This is not surprising, as it had enthralled me ever since I was a small child, since in fact Granny and Grandad Arnold took me when I was four years old to Cambridge's New Theatre – a pretty miniature opera house, now, alas, demolished – to see the pantomime of *Robinson Crusoe*. I was on that occasion somewhat puzzled by what was happening, because we sat in the middle of the dress circle, from which I could not see the stalls; my impression was that there must also have been a second stage downstairs. And the conductor of the orchestra riveted me: I thought he was one of several, mistaking the moving bows of the violinists for further conductors' batons.

My thespian interest grew more fervent at the age of twelve or thirteen, at which time I used to make a point, so far as savings from my pocket money allowed, of seeing all I could of performances of Gilbert and Sullivan operettas during the annual visits to the New Theatre of the D'Oyly Carte Opera Company. It was possible, by queuing for two or three hours, to obtain a good seat in the gallery for a shilling (5p), and by doing this I was able to see three or four performances, or even more, during a week. I saw nearly the whole Gilbert and Sullivan repertory in the course of a year or so. And I saw some superb performers, among whom were Sir Henry Lytton, Bertha Lewis, Darrell Fancourt, Leslie Rands, Sydney Granville, Muriel Dickson and Margery Eyre. I was decidedly in love with Miss Eyre, an attractive mezzo-soprano with a voice that caused shivers to go from end to end of my adolescent spine. Her departure from Cambridge at the end of the 1933 season filled me with despair for weeks.

Most Saturday evenings I went with Auntie Connie to performances at the Festival Theatre on Newmarket Road, where for sixpence (2.5p) we could perch on a bench in the gallery. This, the former Theatre Royal, Barnwell, was an experimental arts theatre, opened in 1926 as the 'most progressive theatre in England'. In the meantime it had been used as a mission hall: a lamp over the stage door still carried the inscription 'All have sinned'. In 1926 its ownership passed to Terence Stannus Gray, a member of the Cambridgeshire gentry, an Egyptologist and theorist of the theatre, much influenced by Edward Gordon Craig, and to Harold Ridge, an authority on advanced stage lighting. The years during which Gray directed the somewhat oddly named Festival Theatre (it had no connexion with any festival), Cambridge had opportunity to see many brilliant if somewhat eccentric productions, conceived on the principle that the most important person in the theatre was not the playwright, not the designer, not the performer, but the producer: Gray set out not to interpret the text of a play, but to 'create an independent work of theatre art'.

As to myself, despite having taken me to see Somerset Maugham's *Rain* when I was five, my parents opined that I was too young at seven to be taken to see Gray's productions, with the result that my knowledge of them is secondhand. But I have read reports and comments, and have seen photographs of many of them. I also have a complete collection of the programmes from those early days, which I acquired in 1939 from David's bookstall for 12s. 6d. (62.5p). What is more, I heard a certain amount about Festival productions from my father, who during the earliest days went to a performance every week. After Gray's initial period, Father must have lost interest, for he rarely entered the place after 1930. Perhaps his interest had been aroused when the building was adapted from its mission-hall days, for the Lister firm made the mechanism for the stage turntable.

Many famous theatre people began their careers at the Festival Theatre, among them Gray's cousin Ninette de Valois (real name Edris Stannus), Flora Robson, Robert Donat, Margaret Rawlings, Robert Morley, Vivienne Bennett and the producer Tyrone Guthrie. When Gray decided that he had for the time being derived enough experience from his theatre, he handed over its direction for a period to the producer, Anmer Hall, and once again, for a season, to another producer, Norman Marshall, after which he returned for a few seasons. He took his final bow in July 1933, when the Festival was leased to Joseph Gordon Macleod, one of Gray's actors. It was soon after Macleod took charge that I began to attend performances.

To judge from early Festival photographs, Macleod's productions were not unlike Gray's, but much less spectacular, for he was not a rich man and was therefore unable to afford the elaborate podia, costumes and effects of his predecessor. Here notwithstanding, a brief walk from our house, a rich theatrical experience was available, enabling me to see *avant garde* theatrical experiment at first hand. I saw some rarely-produced plays, including Shakespeare's *Cymbeline*, produced in a low maze on a slightly tilted floor, Shaw's *Captain Brassbound's Conversion* and *Cyril Comes Over* by H.R. Tomalin, to mention but three.

By 1936 Macleod decided to cut his losses, and left Cambridge for ever. The Festival Theatre never had paid its way, for it was far too small even if it had been full to capacity at every performance, and it was invariably far from full. After Macleod's departure the theatre was closed for a time, but some months later it was leased by yet another director, Alfred Huxley, who, surprisingly enough, did for short time seem to cover his expenses, at least he filled the theatre night after night, and week after week. But this was achieved at considerable artistic sacrifice, for the plays presented were drawing-room comedies, detective mysteries, and farces. I took part in some of them, my evenings being free, and Huxley being short of actors for minor parts. It was fun working with professionals, and I learnt much from my experience, especially about production and lighting.

Huxley had a partner in his enterprise, Frank Harvey junior, a former alumnus of St Catharine's College. He was, I think, an Australian, and later returned home. He was very kind to me and went to great trouble to initiate me into the secrets of make-up. One or two of the rôles I was given portrayed middle-aged men, and at seventeen it was by no means easy to present a convincing appearance. But with Frank's help, all was accomplished.

In 1935 I joined the Rodney Dramatic Club, which was generally considered a cut above the average 'town' amateur group. Its members at this time included Leonard ('Tommy') Thompson, who had recently worked as an understudy to Tom Walls in the Aldwych farces of Ben Travers; he had settled in Cambridge, having, with a friend, taken over Rossiter's Art Shop in Rose Crescent. Another Rodney member contemporary with me was Will Carter, the printer and typographer, and founder of the Rampant Lions Press. I took part in one or two productions, including *If I were King* by Justin McCarthy. I enjoyed the experience, but to me its greatest value lay in the several friendships which ensued, particularly one with a man who remained a close friend until his death in 1972 – H.C.C. ('Dickie') Band, then manager of the old Cambridge firm of bookbinders, John P. Gray and Son. Some of the most fastidious bibliophiles entrusted their books to Dickie for repair and conservation; Sir Geoffrey Keynes, the doyen of them all, spoke of his books as being 'Dickied' when he sent them to Gray's for treatment. For several years Dickie served also as bookbinding adviser to the Bodleian Library at Oxford.

Back at the Festival, Huxley started a supporters' club, and on Sunday evenings presented a number of plays and entertainments for its members. For one of these occasions he allowed me to stage the medieval miracle play *Noye's Fludde* by Don Randle Heggenett; I do not think I made a bad job of producing this rather difficult little play: at any rate it was well received. The setting was a dark blue curtain, with three simple stepped podia. The players were dressed in flowing robes and each wore a cubist mask taken from Terence Gray's old stock which I discovered in a dusty store at the back of the stage. Many years afterwards the play was used as a basis of an opera for children composed by Benjamin Britten.

During the year 1936 the new Arts Theatre on Peas Hill was opened. It was founded by the economist John Maynard Keynes, with the assistance of George ('Dadie') Rylands, the Shakespearean scholar, and Miss J.M. Harvey, for the presentation of the five arts of drama, opera, music, ballet and film – hence its pentagonal logo. Its first general manager called himself N. Openshaw Higgins, which he later simplified to Norman Higgins. It was largely due to Higgins's energy and sense of occasion that for several years after its opening season it was thought stylish to be seen there. Many of the shows were first-class; they included the first performances of Ralph Vaughan Williams's comic operetta *The Poisoned Kiss*, with décor by Gwendolen Raverat and an orchestra conducted by Cyril B. Rootham; a presentation of the Greek play, *The Frogs* of Aristophanes by members of the University; a season of Ibsen, in which Jean Forbes-Robertson appeared in *Hedda Gabler* and Lydia Lopokova (the ballerina and wife of J.M. Keynes) in *A Doll's House*; and there were performances by the Vic-Wells Ballet, the foundation of the present Royal Ballet.

The last was for me the very peak of interest, one which was eventually to steer me into a new and absorbing area of art. On the evening I saw ballet for the first time, the performance included *Carnaval* (in which Ninette de Valois danced – one of her late appearances), *The Rake's Progress*, and Act III of *Casse Noisette*, in which the Sugar Plum Fairy was danced by the ballerina, Mary Honer, who a little later, and for a few years, was to become one of my closest friends. At ballet performances at the Arts, Maynard and Lydia Keynes were usually in their box, and to Lydia, at curtain-call, the dancers gave a special bow or curtsey, an honour usually reserved for royalty, but accorded to her as one of Diaghilev's great ballerinas.

The advent of the Arts Theatre dealt a mortal blow to the Festival Theatre, with its less convenient and rather remote situation. And it must be admitted also that the quality of the productions had fallen off. The public would perhaps have supported the Festival if its presentations had warranted it, but the type of play it was currently producing proved neither sufficiently attractive nor sufficiently interesting. Huxley terminated his lease, and there were between 1936 and 1940 sporadic attempts by various companies to revive interest in the Festival, in which, as in Huxley's time, I took part. But, all in all, it was a sad end to what had for a short period been one of the most interesting and significant movements in the English theatre.

****

All this time I continued to paint, although I had so far produced little of artistic consequence. But more feeling appeared in my work after, at the age of nineteen, I had for the first time fallen deeply in love. I had been in love before, but these earlier affairs of the heart, while pleasant enough, were quickly over, ending in inevitable disillusion. This time it seemed different, but it ended after ten months, when my sweetheart perceived that it would not do: temperamentally we were light-years apart, and our ideas and beliefs were totally opposed. But while it lasted, it was as dizzy, as intense as anything described by Keats in *Endymion*.

Its termination left me desolate for a time, yet the experience of such deep nostalgia aided my art, and prompted me to express in my miniature paintings a green and mossy world, with swans, and here and there balletic lovers dancing *adagios* against a background of mountains, trees and lakes by moonlight, dominated by melancholy blues and sad greens, and highlighted with gold or silver where moonbeams played on shadowy and ivy-shrouded forms.

Apart from this visual expression, I was too fiercely proud to admit to the depths of my unhappiness and regret, and I endeavoured, I am sure successfully, to give an impression of carefree abandon. Still, I badly needed to love and to be loved: the reality of that came several years later, and then it brought with it depths of mutual devotion, affection and true happiness such as I had never before considered possible, let alone experienced. But at the time of which I am writing my future love, still a little girl at school, was unknown to me. My quest for her was to be long and exhausting; would that I had known that, however far into the future, I should one day attain and experience, through her and with her, William Blake's 'Soft Moony Universe, feminine, lovely, Pure, mild and gentle'!

81

Let those who must sneer at young love. To the adolescent it is real enough, heartbreaking enough to plunge a boy or girl into despair, even suicide. Romeo and Juliet, Aucassin and Nicolette, Pelléas and Mélisande, Tristan and Isolde, Young Werther – these are victims of love who all too vividly recall the searing pains and spiritual hopelessness of disappointed young ardour.

Seven
Ballet and Other Matters

I completed my apprenticeship in March 1939. Some eighteen months before that I had begun to indulge my growing preoccupation with the composite art of ballet, reading all I could of its history and appreciation, and seeing performances whenever I had the opportunity. My limited resources, suitably garnered, allowed me a number of trips to London for performances of the two Ballet Russe companies – the Covent Garden Russian Ballet and the Ballet Russe de Monte Carlo at Drury Lane – and of their predecessor, Colonel de Basil's Ballet Russe.

Although since those days I have seen an enormous amount of ballet, I have never seen more exciting performances than those given by these Russian companies; I have, on the other hand, seen very many worse. Their performances overshadowed anything contemporary English companies could offer, with a whole galaxy of stars. Léonide Massine, one of the greatest choreographic geniuses of the twentieth century, and one of the best of all character dancers, had reached the apogee of his powers. His *Gaîté Parisienne*, with music by Offenbach and costumes and décor by Comte Etienne de Beaumont, was a highlight of the 1938 season. I saw one of its early performances, with Massine himself dancing the leading rôle, a rich and womanising Peruvian out to enjoy the delights of Paris, being swirled around in a froth of midinettes, cocodettes, and a most attractive *corps de ballet* of can-can girls. I found it stimulating beyond description, like nothing I had previously seen; it was one of many strong influences that swept me into an overwhelming balletomania during the following few years.

In the seasons of 1938 and 1939, several brilliant ballerinas performed. Apart from guest artistes, the most senior was Alexandra Danilova, one of Diaghilev's last ballerinas and one of the last ballerinas trained under the *ancien régime*, in days when expense and time were of no account. Her perfect technique, united with a highly sensitive temperament and a perfectly proportioned physique, made a wonderful combination. Her interpretation of Odette, the enchanted princess in the attenuated one-act version of *Le Lac des Cygnes*, was dominated by a sense of impending and inexorable tragedy.

But for feminine allure could there ever have been such an enchanting dancer as Irina Baronova, who at the incredibly early age of thirteen was a star ballerina? By the time I first saw Baronova she had already become, although only eighteen, a fully mature dancer with a breathtaking technique, yet she still retained the dewy, apple-blossom freshness and gaiety which had been her hallmarks as a young girl. To me Irina was a ballerina to perfection. And not only to me, for Anton Dolin described her as among the finest ballerinas he had partnered, saying that her *joie de vivre* was the nearest in her generation to that of Lydia Lopokova.

I learned also that she was something more: despite her youth she was (like two other young contemporary ballerinas, Tatiana Riabouchinska and Tamara Toumanova) a link with the past, a living affirmation of the continuity of her art. Her teacher was one of the greatest Russian ballerinas turned out by the Imperial School in St. Petersburg, Olga Preobrazhenskaya, who had herself learned the great classical rôles from their creators, Marius Petipa and Lev Ivanov. Through these and their predecessors Irina had an unbroken artistic pedigree extending back into the early years of the 18th century; she also enjoyed the advantage of learning 20th-century ballets direct from their creators: Michel Fokine, Léonide Massine, Georges Balanchine, Bronislava Nijinska and others. Thus her interpretations carried an authority which few outside the Ballet Russe could even begin to emulate. It is good to know that she is still passing on that knowledge to dancers of the late 20th century.

After the outbreak of war in 1939 we in England saw no more of the Ballet Russe, and my balletic interests of necessity became largely occupied by the work of English companies, particularly the Vic-Wells and the Rambert. The Ballet Rambert visited Cambridge quite often during the War, once in the Festival Theatre during one of its ephemeral later administrations, and thereafter at the Arts. Its repertoire included perfect miniature ballets, typified by the very English *Lady into Fox* (1939; choreography by Andrée Howard), based on David Garnett's novel about the strange metamorphosis of his heroine, Mrs Tebrick, into a vixen.

Nevertheless, Marie Rambert did bring something of the Russian tradition to English ballet, for she had been a member of Diaghilev's company, and had taught eurhythmics to Nijinsky. Known affectionately as 'Mim' she was one of the warmest and most exuberant characters it has been my good fortune to meet. She thought nothing of turning cartwheels in the street after a party, and had a ready anecdote to suit every occasion. She was one of the least pompous people I have ever known.

Balletomania of necessity took second place to my unspectacular activities in the war effort. For its first three years I worked on the production of apparatus for what was then known as radio-location, but has since acquired the more concise name of radar; for its last three years I was employed on making lighting plants for the Admiralty. I became bored by the often repetitive nature of the work, and volunteered first for the Navy and later for the Army, but each time I was told firmly to get on with what I was doing, so I bothered no further and enjoyed to my heart's content what ballet I could see.

I had become especially attracted to a German *émigré* company which I had seen several times before the War at the Arts Theatre in Cambridge: Ballets Jooss, a highly original company, directed by Kurt Jooss, who had studied under the great dance innovator and philosopher, Rudolf von Laban. Jooss, a German refugee whose school was then based at Dartington Hall, near Totnes in Devon, took what he wanted from the technique of the classical ballet, eschewing what he saw as its more artificial elements such as dancing *sur les pointes*, and combined it with the Laban system, which sought to express through the natural movements of human physique all aspects and nuances of the human psyche.

Jooss's masterly choreography ranged from the delightful Biedermeier confection of *A Ball in Old Vienna* (1932) to political commentaries like his masterpiece *The Green Table* (1932), a modern dance of death which begins and ends with a group of frock-coated statesmen arguing around a green-topped table; between these two scenes war breaks out, and Death is unleashed, contaminating everybody and everything. Yet if truth must be told, there was a certain monotony in some of Jooss's ballets. They often seemed too weighty, and in some cases their plots were far too complicated to be expressed in dance. *Chronica* (1939; based on an Italian Renaissance theme) was so involved that it was impossible to follow its plot without the help of a long and detailed synopsis. No doubt much of the *gravitas* of these ballets was due to the menacing era of growing threat and, in the end, the onset of world war; but the point was driven home so hard in Jooss's progressive work that it was often blunted.

Elsewhere, when Jooss allowed his humour full rein, he showed that he did not allow political and social problems to monopolise his genre. He demonstrated this in the fairy-tale ballets *Seven Heroes* (1937) and *A Spring Tale* (1939) and by *Company at the Manor* (1943), the last-named as if Jane Austen were being expressed in dance. By the end of the War others had begun to choreograph works for Jooss: Sigurd Leeder in the comedy-ballet *Sailor's Fancy* (1943) and Hans Züllig in the romantic *Le Bosquet* (1945). In this aspect of his company's work, Jooss had an asset which gave him a perspective beyond many other Modern Dance choreographers, such as Martha Graham whose otherwise brilliant work lacked one important component: laughter.

Some dancers in the Ballets Jooss would have shone in any company: such were Hans Züllig, with a virtuoso technique comparable with that of the great Stanislas Idzikowski; and the beautiful Dutch girl, Noelle de Mosa, whose feminine grace brought both joy and pathos to many of the Jooss presentations.

Whatever the impact of Jooss and his ballets – and do not misunderstand me, despite a few reservations I admired them –

Upper: Myself aged about 6 months, with my mother and father on the beach at Great Yarmouth, 1919.

Lower: John and Annie Elizabeth Arnold, my maternal grandparents, with their family, about 1909. *Standing:* My mother, Uncle Jack. *At Front:* Uncle Tom, Auntie Connie, Auntie Ruby, Auntie Hilda.

Upper: Frances Emily Lister, my grandmother.

Lower: George Lister, my grandfather. Both about 1905.

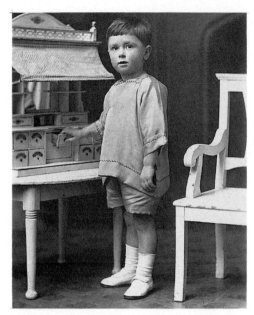

Upper: Myself aged about 4 years.

Lower: Uncle Humphrey Lant, 1929.

Upper: Ernie Fox operating a centre-lathe, about 1960.

Lower: Wrought iron panel from Castle Howard, Yorkshire conserved in the workshops of George Lister and Sons Ltd., about 1955.

Silhouette portrait by myself of Albert Cousins, 1952.

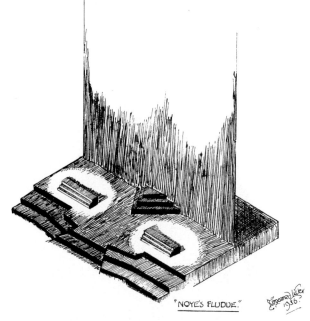

"NOYE'S FLUDDE."

Upper: Design for setting by myself for *Noye's Fludde*, produced at the Festival Theatre, Cambridge, 1936.

Lower: Myself (standing in overalls, centre left) as 'Numero Quinze' in *Libel!* by Edward Wooll. The Festival Repertory Company, 1939. Festival Theatre, Cambridge.

Myself, 1939.

Irina Baronova, 1938.

Mary Honer and Leslie Edwards in *Coppélia*, Act II, 1940.
Photo. Gordon Anthony. From the collections of
the Theatre Museum. By courtesy of the Board of
Trustees of the Victoria and Albert Museum.

9

Kurt Jooss, about 1938.
Photo. Gordon Anthony. From the collections of
the Theatre Museum. By courtesy of the Board of
Trustees of the Victoria and Albert Museum.

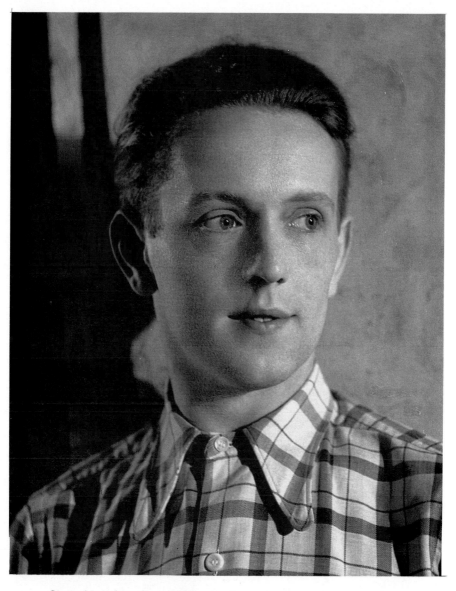

Sigurd Leeder, about 1935.

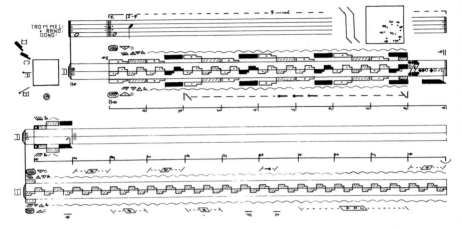

SCHNEEFLOCKENSPIEL.
KINDERSPIEL FÜR 4 GRUPPEN.
Von JENNY GERTZ.

Upper: Snowflake Play. Children's Game for four groups by Jenny Gertz. Opening movements recorded in Kinetography Laban, about 1936.

Lower: Two pupils of Jenny Gertz in the open-air theatre at Dartington Hall, Devon, about 1939.

Selma Burger

Left: Cover of programme of dance recital, arranged by myself, 1941.

Right: Selma Burger, about 1937.

Pamela and myself, just married, 1947.

Three miniature paintings
by myself.

Upper left:
Fionnuala flying over
Moyle, 1945.
   Private Collection.

Upper right:
The Unicorn of the
Marshes, 1947.
   Brotherton Collection,
   University of Leeds.

Lower:
The Three Swans, 1956.
   Private Collection.

15

Two wood-engravings by myself:

Upper: Church and Crescent Moon, 1956.

Lower: Yggdrasil, 1958.

Two miniature paintings by myself.

Upper: Hindu Dancer, 1952. Diploma Collection, Royal Society of Miniature Painters, Sculptors and Gravers.

Lower: Hortus Conclusus, 1978. Collection of the late Arnold Fawcus, Paris.

Myself with Pamela and Rory (aged about 12 months) and
Arthur Astbury, 1953.

Philip Gosse, 1957.

Siegfried Sassoon with friend, May 1952.

Upper: My father, about 1968.

Lower: My mother, about 1968.

Myself with Simon Lissim, about 1960.

Rory and Delia entertaining us, Christmas 1964.

A group of books, most published by the Golden Head Press,
designed by myself.

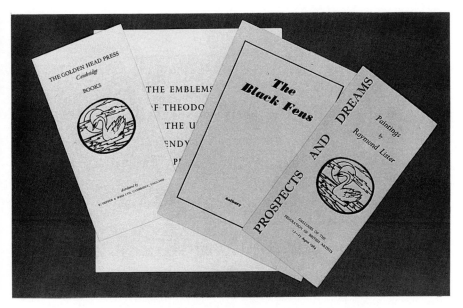

The Golden Head Press and other ephemera.

Rudolf von Laban, about 1934.

Upper: The Chamber Idyll by Edward Calvert.
Wood-engraving, 1831.

Lower: Harvest under a Crescent Moon by Samuel Palmer.
Wood-engraving, *circa* 1826.

Upper: The Sleeping Shepherd by Samuel Palmer, Etching, 1857.

Lower: Illustration by William Blake, for Virgil's First Eclogue, from Robert John Thornton's *Pastorals of Virgil.* Wood-engraving, 1821.

Myself selecting (from photographs) works by Samuel Palmer
for *Samuel Palmer and 'The Ancients'*, a major exhibition held at
the Fitzwilliam Museum, Cambridge, 1984. Courtesy of
Cambridge Evening News.

Myself with Sir Geoffrey Keynes (Samuel Palmer looking on in the background), at the opening of the exhibition *Samuel Palmer: A Vision Recaptured*, Victoria and Albert Museum, 1978.

Upper: Myself and Pamela at Linton, on the day I had received my Litt.D., 1990.

Lower: Myself with Irina Baronova in our Cambridge garden, 1992.

Pamela, about 1986.

I found their intellectual base stimulating, and I set out to learn all I could of Jooss's major theoretical source, the theories of Laban; I began to accomplish this during 1941. Jooss and Sigurd Leeder, his *maître de ballet*, had been interned on the Isle of Man in 1940 with other 'enemy' aliens, during the scare of a possible invasion and of possible fifth-columnists. The threat having abated, they were released and Jooss re-established his ballet in Cambridge, which was a piece of luck for me. I was a guest at a small dinner-party given in honour of Jooss and his wife in the Arts Theatre Restaurant, and was there introduced to him by Camille Prior, a local lady *au courant* with theatrical matters.

Jooss seemed a very serious man and smiled rarely, and then almost secretly. The first thing one noticed about him was his enormous head, a great dome, the size of which at this period was further exaggerated by an immense mane of frothy hair which reached his shoulders and grew outwards and behind like a smoky grey-black halo. He was of medium build, small even; his hands were plump, almost feminine, almost too aesthetic, and he wore an effeminate-looking gold ring with a bright blue stone on his finger. His nails were too long for my taste. The one person who was able to coax a ready laugh from him was Marie Rambert, who would stand up after his lectures to the University Ballet Club and say in her strong Polish accent: 'I wish to contradict all you have been saying!' and then tear at his Modern Dance theories like a terrier at a rat. 'She is a great little fighter', said Jooss admiringly. Jooss's wife Aino (Siimola) was an Estonian, very elegant, but, like her husband, rather distant in manner. When I met her again many years later, she could not have been more affable, so perhaps maturity had brought some mellowing of her character (or perhaps it had made *me* more agreeable).

I mentioned to Jooss how interested I had become in his work and in Laban's theories, and asked how I could learn more about them. 'Why don't you speak to Leeder?' he replied. 'He adores teaching and I am sure he would be willing to give you some lessons.' He asked me to visit him one evening at his house in Clarkson Road, when he would introduce us. Having duly presented myself, I was both impressed and surprised to see in a prominent position on the drawing-room wall, a miniature of Marie Taglioni, for Jooss had discarded so much of what Marie personified: the ephemeral Sylphide, gliding over the stage *sur les pointes*.

I liked Sigurd Leeder immediately: a much more extravert personality than the somewhat dour Jooss, very humorous, with a sharp sense of fun. I suppose with his blond hair and bright blue eyes he would have been considered a first-class Aryan by the Nazis, but Sigurd would have laughed at the idea with scorn. I soon found him erudite in almost every aspect of the theatre and its history. He had brought with him to Cambridge a small library of books on the dance, which despite its size, was of superlative quality. It encompassed every imaginable aspect of the subject, from sixteenth-century monographs to the most modern treatises on ballet and related arts.

Sigurd readily agreed to give me a weekly lesson at his flat in Bene't Street, above what was then the Friar House Restaurant, lessons that were also to develop into a valued friendship which was only interrupted when my war work called me away from Cambridge. Sigurd went abroad after the War, and we lost contact. But in those dark wartime days he helped to lighten my heart by instructing me in the rudiments of choreutics (the theoretical principles and harmonies of the body's orientation in space, based on the icosahedron, a twenty-faced solid figure), eukinetics (the dynamic structure of movements), and kinetography (dance notation). Needless to say, full-time study would hardly have been sufficient if I were to assimilate all of this, but Sigurd was an inspired teacher, with an eager pupil, and within some fifty weekly lessons I learnt much that has enabled me to understand many aspects of human movement – physical, psychological, aesthetic – the existence of which I should otherwise hardly have suspected.

Of kinetography (now often called Labanotation), I found it an exciting experience to realise how all human movement, its rhythms, tensions and harmonics, and not only ballet and dance, could be written down for posterity. Dance notation still fascinates me; when I was learning about it from Sigurd, it remained a closed book to most people, and friends in the ballet to whom I spoke of it refused to believe in the practicality of any notation: a scepticism that survives even now here and there, though its use and study have now been widely disseminated, thanks especially to one of its leading exponents, Ann Hutchinson. And the Royal Ballet, within the last three or four decades has adopted notation, using a system invented by Rudolf Benesh; so far as I have been able to judge it is not so minutely accurate as kinetography, but the fact that it is being used at all demonstrates its practicality. In Russia, V.I. Stepanov's system of notation, based on music notation, has been in use since Tsarist times; Léonide Massine used it to illustrate points in his book *Massine on Choreography* (1976). The Israelis, Noa Eshkol, an authority on dance gymnastics who studied under Sigurd Leeder, and Abraham Wachmann, an architect, developed in the 1950s a system based on the idea of each joint of the body being contained within an imaginary sphere. It has a logical mathematical basis and is used widely, especially in Israel. I had myself experimented with such an idea, and still have some notes I made about it during the 1940s.

I have always believed the historical perspective of any subject to be of prime importance: if its current state of development is to be fully understood, its foundations and subsequent evolvement must also be comprehended. Dance notation is no exception, so I set about learning what I could of its history, beginning with the system invented by Charles-Louis Beauchamps at about the end of the seventeenth century. In this I was helped by the musicologist, Charles Cudworth, who had access to many libraries and music collections. He arranged for me to consult rare works such as Raoul-Auger Feuillet's *Recueil de Danses* (Paris, 1704), which I laboriously transcribed page by page and plate by plate; Kellom Tomlinson's beautiful *The Art of Dancing* (1735), which depicts dances in progress with notations of the movements marked on the floor; and Friedrich Albert Zorn's *Grammar of the Art of Dancing* (Boston, Mass., 1905).

A year or so after I had begun my studies with Sigurd, I was introduced to Ninette de Valois at a dinner party in Cambridge. Somebody mentioned my interest in notation and she asked me to tell her about it. She was not an easy woman to talk to, as she continually interrupted me, and ran ahead of what I was trying to say, and despite her expressed interest, did not seem anxious to listen to my views. When I finally got around to saying something, I recommended kinetography as a suitable medium for recording the repertoire of the Vic-Wells Ballet. Many years later, in 1954, she described kinetography as a 'wonderful new system' – it had existed since 1928! – but in the event she decided to use the Benesh system.

Following closely on my interest in Laban, I became curious to know more of the work of Oskar Schlemmer, one of the artists who worked with Walter Gropius at the Bauhaus in Weimar. I was struck by photographs and reports of his dance presentations, such as the *Triadic Ballet* (1922), and of his analyses of human physique and movement. True, Schlemmer's methods and conclusions are of a different emphasis from those of Laban, but one is nevertheless forcibly reminded of the similarities in the working of each man's mind.

One is reminded also of the wide vision of Renaissance man, for Schlemmer had the same investigative and experimental approach to the structure, design and dynamics of the human figure as that applied to so many areas in Leonardo da Vinci's notebooks. They are somewhat related also to the designs in a curious little book of engravings published in Florence in 1624: *Bizzarie di varie figure di Giovanni Battista Bracelli pittore fiorentino.* In each of Bracelli's plates (with but one or two exceptions), two related anthropomorphous figures are depicted, variously constructed of frames, leaves, boxes, rings, geometrical surfaces and so forth: some seem to afford even a prevision of Cubism. Similarly, some of Schlemmer's figures are constructed of rings, cubes, and other solids, and one wonders if he might have seen the Bracelli engravings. They are, however, designed with different ends in view: Bracelli was attempting fantasy, Schlemmer analysis.

****

I was in 1940 introduced to the brilliant virtuoso ballerina of the Vic-Wells Ballet, Mary Honer, after a performance at the Arts Theatre. She was a tiny woman, with a bright eager face and a pretty voice, and naturally I was immediately smitten. She said the Company would shortly be going to Brighton and it happened that I too had to go there in connection with my work, so I asked her if I might look her up, and we arranged to meet at the theatre after the closing performance on Saturday evening. Within half an hour of the final curtain we were sitting in the lounge of the Old Ship Hotel, having a *tête-à-tête* over a bottle of wine, confessing intimacies and exchanging views on the ballet. She had, she told me, been married to Harold Turner, one of England's finest virtuoso dancers; I had in fact heard about this, to say nothing of the maltreatment she had suffered during this ill-starred marriage.

Mary said she was shortly going with the Ballet to Holland to dance in a series of performances in various towns, including Rotterdam. When I saw her back to her lodgings, I pressed into her hand a tiny iron horseshoe that I had bought some years earlier at Cockington in Devon, and told her I hoped it would bring her good luck on the trip. Poor Mary! She badly needed any luck my little horseshoe might bring her, for the German invasion of the Low Countries began while the Ballet was in Rotterdam, and they escaped miraculously, embarking for home in the midst of bombs and bullets. As soon as she arrived in England she sent me a letter, which began, 'Your wee horseshoe certainly brought me luck!'

I saw much of her after this, and, through her, got to know many other members of the company. One of the coryphées had a boyfriend who composed limericks, and he presented this one to Mary and me:

> A young ballerina named Honer
> Had plenty of men to enthrone her.
> When her heart was vacated
> She quickly located
> A Ray-dio expert to own her.

Mary came to ballet from musical comedy, yet her training in ballet had been impeccable, for she had studied under Judith Espinosa, Margaret Craske, and under two Imperial Russian dancers Nicolas Legat and Lyubov Egorova. In technique alone Mary Honer was star material, but her chubby physique, feminine and attractive no doubt, lacked the willowy arabesque so essential in the great classical rôles. As a comedienne she was at her best in *Coppélia* – in 1940 she became the first English ballerina to dance the part of Swanilda in its entirety – and as the Bride, a rôle she created in 1937, in that effervescent *morceau* of English mischief, Ashton's *A Wedding Bouquet:* in such rôles her physique proved a decided advantage.

Always popular in the Company, she never gave way to tantrums, always a good trouper, but this very lack of temperamental dynamism detracted from her very real qualities as a dancer. I remember her annoyance when a critic referred to her as the 'ever dependable Mary Honer'. Even so, that was her virtue, and it was one of her tragedies that she hankered after Odette and Giselle, when she was so completely brilliant as Swanilda and the Sugar Plum Fairy.

Mr and Mrs Leonard Knight Elmhirst, founders of the Dartington Hall Trust, invited the Vic-Wells Ballet to spend Christmas 1940 at Dartington to rest after a hard year's work. I decided I would join Mary there, and booked into a hotel at Totnes. The Elmhirsts very kindly invited me to join the ballet at meals, which meant that I could be with Mary most of the time. We took meals on refectory tables in the old hall, and estate workers and their families sat down with us; it was all very pleasant, and reminiscent of the old, now departed pastoral world.

Among other guests of the Elmhirsts, I encountered a dark-haired woman of surly and forbidding appearance who seemed incapable of common courtesy, for she snubbed almost everybody who approached her. She was Beryl de Zoete, an authority on Balinese dancing and drama, and the mistress for many years of Arthur Waley, the brilliant translator of Chinese poetry. Waley, though not a member, had close connections with the Bloomsbury Circle, some of whose cold arrogance had rubbed off on to the uncomely Beryl.

Mary Honer and I viewed our relationship in different ways and with different ends in view; if we had taken that into account from the beginning we might have saved ourselves much future disappointment and distress. As always I was very romantic, but Mary wanted reassurance after her short, unhappy marriage and divorce. She wanted children more than anything, she told me, and many times we talked of marrying. But before long we began to grate on each other and realised that we should become incompatible partners. Our outlook, our opinions, our personalities: everything clashed. Almost every time we met, trouble quickly developed, and ended in my drinking excessively, which in turn caused her to mount her moral high horse. This was one of the contradictions in her character, for at one time she would show unmistakably her rigid Lowland Presbyterian code, inherited no doubt from her Scottish mother, then at another she would relate bawdy jokes. As to drinking, she enjoyed tipsy occasions, but would regret it next morning and lay the blame at my door. Time and time again we became reconciled, only to fall out once more.

Our last *grand rapprochement* began in 1942 after several months of estrangement following a quarrel, during a northern tour of the Ballet in 1941, after a dinner party at Manchester, given by Jean Bedells, a soloist in the Ballet, to celebrate her birthday. Difficulties had arisen a few days previously at Harrogate, and in an endeavour to sweeten the situation I had presented Mary with a pair of earrings she had admired in the window of an antique shop. The gift had been received ungraciously, and, as might have been expected in the circumstances, I had spent an hour or two drinking in a pub near the Pump Room, which resulted in the usual recriminations. The quarrel continued at Manchester, and well into the night after the Bedells party. When I got back to Cambridge I decided that it would be best for both of us if we called it a day, so I wrote and told her so, and broke off the affair.

Some months afterwards, in 1942, she was appearing as Swanilda in *Coppélia* at the Arts Theatre. I took a small party to see the performance, and without doubt Mary danced as brilliantly as at any time in her career. After the show I gave a dinner in the Arts Theatre Restaurant, mainly to reciprocate Jean Bedells's hospitality at Manchester, so she was one of the guests, accompanied by John Hart, another member of the Company. Mary, unbeknown to me, was also dining in the restaurant with friends. I did not notice her until, as we were leaving, she hurried after me, calling, 'Hello, Ray!' An appropriate bouquet delivered to her dressing room next day clinched yet another reconciliation.

Mary was going to Porlock for a holiday, and would I care to join her there? The idea appealed to me, and we spent several happy days fishing in Porlock Bay and pony-trekking in the 'Doone Valley', taking in some of the ambience of R.D. Blackmore's novel. But before the end of the week my earlier apprehensions had been fully confirmed and I knew that nothing worthwhile would ever develop between us. For a year or two we continued to see one another intermittently, but even friendship diminished, and after the middle of 1945 I never saw her again.

Ill-luck dogged her. At the peak of her career she succumbed to athlete's heart and, soon after that, de Valois stopped her from dancing big rôles and appointed her a ballet mistress. I feel sure that Ninette's intentions were good, believing the strain of major rôles would be detrimental to Mary's health, might even kill her. But she resented it – perhaps understandably, for it came as an anti-climax after the glamour of her earlier career – and she soon took her leave of the Vic-Wells Ballet to become a 'straight' actress in Shakespearean rôles at the Open Air Theatre in Regent's Park. She never again set the Thames on fire; as an actress she was good, but had no gift in this art to compare with her dancing. Some years after this she joined the Embassy Ballet formed in 1945 by Molly Lake and her husband Travis Kemp. She made one last triumphant appearance in 1950 in her old rôle as the Bride in *A Wedding Bouquet* at a twenty-first anniversary gala at Covent Garden.

She married the actor Peter M. Bell, whom she met after beginning her new career. I heard that she had the child she longed for and I hope she found real happiness in her remaining time, for (again that ill-luck) she died in 1965 when she was only fifty-one after a long and painful illness.

****

The years 1940 and 1941 were not propitious for the arts, but I have never been able to put them aside whatever the circumstances and in what little spare time I could find, I formed an amateur dance group. The idea really grew out of a concert given on 5 March 1940, which I arranged in Houghton Hall in Cambridge, then a well-equipped little theatre, now part of St. Alban's School in Union Road. The event was in aid of the Red Cross, to which I afterwards handed a handsome sum; it consisted of instrumental music, singing and recitations, and concluded with the presentation of a little play in verse which I had written when I was seventeen, a pastiche in the genre of the mediaeval miracle play, entitled *Saint George*. It told the story of Princess Sabra and the Dragon (dressed and made up to look like Hitler!) and her rescuer, St. George. It was a simple work, but effective, and the audience seemed to like it. I had the idea of staging it in two movements: mime and mime-dialogue, with the first movement in dumbshow to music from Grieg and the second without music, but in verse dialogue.

The mime was especially well received, and it suggested to me that if we could only extend our amateur talent somewhat we might be able to present some stylised *avant-garde* dance-dramas. One of our circle knew a young refugee who had been a *coryphée* at the Munich State Opera. Selma Burger had been a pupil of Heinrich Kröller (1880-1930); she was Jewish, but had the good fortune to escape from Germany. Selma agreed to supervise weekly classes without pay, and we planned to charge each pupil a small sum to cover the hire of the class-room. Before we could begin I had to work hard, scrubbing the floor, cleaning the walls and fixing up a barre and mirror.

At the well-attended inaugural meeting I expounded my ideas; before it closed I found a nucleus of prospective pupils for Selma's classes. The local newspaper sent a reporter to write an account of our intentions. A fortuitous result of this was that it initiated a lifelong friendship, for the reporter, Arthur K. Astbury, and I found that we had much in common and, perhaps even more important, much to argue about. While he remained in Cambridge Arthur publicised my activities. Over the years he has joined in some of my ventures, sometimes as participant, sometimes as an amused onlooker, and sometimes as a valued critic. He has become 'one of the family', and a more-than-honorary uncle to our children.

Soon after the launching of our classes, another refugee

friend, Arpad Rosner, who had worked in the theatre of Emil Burian in Prague, suggested that I should also arrange classes in Laban's Modern Dance methods. Luckily, he said, one of Laban's former pupils and a noted teacher, Jenny Gertz, was now living in England where she had sought refuge, not because of her race, but because of her communist politics. She had recently been teaching in the junior school at Dartington Hall. Jenny, a typical German with steel-blue eyes and a mass of grey curly hair, agreed to give classes in Modern Dance (which in her case was expressed in what she called a 'moving chorus') on the same terms as those I had agreed with Selma. Kurt Jooss came to see one or two of Jenny's earlier classes, so I felt that by engaging her we had at least achieved some prestige.

In Jenny's moving chorus, the dancers were divided into two groups, one on each side of the stage, each responding or reacting to the movements and tensions of the other in a kind of chiasmus. It was surprisingly effective, especially in the case of children, who were completely uninhibited. Much of it was extemporised, but in such a way that only those who had been properly taught could take part in it. Jenny trained her pupils in various bodily tensions and movements, which they could relate spontaneously from group to group. For instance one group would reach out with their arms gently extended towards the second group, who would react by reaching towards the first; or if the first group had reached forward with strongly tensed arms, the second might fall away as if attacked. This perhaps sounds as if it were simple and uninspired, but more often than not it was incredibly beautiful, especially when performed to music or even to simple percussion. In passing, it is interesting to note that the figures in Bracelli's *Bizzarie*, mentioned earlier, are reacting to one another in much the same way.

For a long time the two sets of ballet and Modern Dance classes flourished and developed, and in March 1941 Jenny's moving chorus was demonstrated at the Amateur Dramatic Club Theatre in Park Street, Cambridge. A more ambitious programme was presented in May at Houghton Hall. The first part was divided between Selma's and Jenny's performers, and the second given over to a group of professional dancers who had worked together at the Jooss-Leeder School of Dance at Dartington, and were now grouped around the composer and pianist Clifton Parker, and the Dutch dancer Yoma Sasburg. Their decidedly *avant-garde* ideas chimed in well with our own.

In addition to our classes and performances, we tried, by means of frequent talks on ballet and dance, painting and music, to arouse interest in our aims. In attempts to raise funds, several successful ballroom dances were organised. In June 1941 we mounted an exhibition of paintings, drawings and sculpture at the Heffer Art Gallery in Cambridge. We did not sell much, but we were able at least to show the work of nine artists including Marjorie Sherlock. And there were several paintings by John Hensher, a friend later closely involved with our group.

But circumstances turned against us, and as the demands of war became more rigorous, support for the ballet classes began to evaporate. Also I found Jenny Gertz ever more demanding and difficult to please. I was young – twenty-two – high-minded and immature. Jenny was in her fifties with strongly-held views, many completely opposed to my own in almost everything. It became very one-sided and she was not prepared to compromise. I had not realised the intensity of her fanatical communism or I would never have agreed to collaborate with her: I found it galling to find her taking up the position that everything Stalin did was right, and that the rest of us were wrong. Later, after the War, Laban told me she had by then even discarded all her previously-held ideas and had devoted herself to teaching classical ballet, because ballet was of such importance in Soviet art.

Years later, in 1961, I saw Jooss again when he was visiting Cambridge with Aino. I spoke to him of Jenny and he said (which by then I already knew) that she was an ungrateful soul, and although a clever and gifted teacher with original ideas, was not on the whole a good influence on her child pupils; he agreed with me that she seemed to have an hypnotic effect on them. He said he had not been at all pleased to find her living in Cambridge, and this no doubt accounted for his somewhat reserved attitude towards me at that time, since it was I who had brought her there. When I spoke to him of my disillusion, he said, 'But you were young and idealistic'. I suppose that sums it up.

Quite apart from Jenny's predatory attitude and political bigotry, support for her classes had dwindled, so I had to tell her that she could not continue. The *coup de grâce* to this first period of the group arrived when in 1942 I was ordered to move nearer to London, to work on Admiralty contracts. I felt that we had achieved a little – a very little – in that we had spread the message that the arts mattered, even in wartime; I believe that our success might have been complete in normal times and circumstances.

I was just over twenty-three when I moved from Cambridge. I worked for twelve hours most days, but apart from that my life was my own, and after work I had plenty of time to reflect on the value of what I had been doing. But in 1942, whatever the seductions of a quieter life, I soon felt restless and again began to toy with the idea of gathering together a group of dancers and artists working to a common end. I managed to get home to Cambridge most weekends, and I thought something could be started, even if temporarily, laying a foundation for expansion after the War. John Hensher agreed to collaborate, and contributed the original idea that we should ultimately revolve our activities around a central artistic laboratory, to explore new ideas and tendencies in the arts.

Being away from Cambridge most of the time made it difficult to keep my finger continuously on the pulse of the activities. Notwithstanding, with John's collaboration the group managed quite well, but the things we did were unfortunately limited in their effect, first because of wartime conditions, and second because we were offering the public something for which they were in no way prepared. In war, most people tend to be more conservative, even reactionary, in their attitudes and tastes than during normal times; untried ideas are disturbing and the public is suspicious of anything new or 'foreign'. So strong was this attitude, and so unusual were the things we were offering, that few bothered to support them.

We arranged two professional theatrical events. One of these was a series of three performances by the German-born husband and wife dance duo, Ernst and Lotte Berk. Ernst was Max Reinhart's choreographer at Salzburg, and had also worked for the Mask Theatre. For this performance we hired the A.D.C.

Theatre, but managed to sell only about a quarter of the available seats. We had taken enormous trouble and had spent much on publicity: John had been to London to attend the Berks' rehearsals so as to prepare for stage management; everything had been planned to the smallest detail. But the public simply stayed away, despite the Berks' superb artistic offering: they combined in their dancing the new tendencies conceived by Laban, Jooss and Mary Wigman (under whom Ernst had studied for a time), with conspicuous elements taken from the traditions of Tibetan, Hindu and other exotic schools of dancing. (Apropos of this, Ernst was much admired by de Zoete.)

Despite this failure, John and I decided to make one more attempt and mounted a lecture-recital of Indian music and singing in a hall in the centre of Cambridge. We engaged first-class exponents, who included Narayana Menon, then music adviser to the Eastern Service of the B.B.C., who had played for Rafiq Anwar's dance troupe. Their impeccable performance was attended by a mere handful of people; it is galling to think that if the recital were to be given now, with wide interest in all kinds of ethnic art, the house would probably be sold out.

The second failure persuaded me to terminate such ventures; I had reached the end of my savings and in any case did not wish to sacrifice more, even if I had it. We did arrange a number of private lectures on music, dancing and painting, which were held in John's commodious drawing room, and they achieved a limited success. But lectures alone could not provide a sufficient outlet for what I had dreamed of.

Just one other thing came out of this second period: a short book in two parts I had written, on a colour theory I had evolved, and on the Modern Dance. Published by the group in 1943 in a very limited edition, it took the form of a Platonic dialogue, all very well in its way, but quite unsuitable for what was, after all, a textbook. The colour theory now looks like mere fumbling in a thick fog, but the exposition of Laban's theories, while somewhat shallow, was not at all bad as a modest introduction, and at that time was the only of them account in English.

****

On the breakdown of my theatrical plans, I turned back with redoubled energy and enthusiasm to miniature painting and applied my mind to assessing its demands, aims and virtues. The miniature is not necessarily a portrait in little. The tradition of miniature in the representation of other subjects (or 'histories' as they used to be called) is much longer, much more widespread. Subject miniatures were in use throughout the history of illuminated manuscripts, which were frequently illustrated by them; they flourished in Persia and Turkey for centuries, also in India where they are still painted. If one is to allow the term 'miniature' to include arts outside paintings (which some purists would not allow), its spirit is present in certain small engravings by such masters as Barthel Beham, Wenzel Hollar, Giulio Bonasone and others, and in more recent manifestations of engraving, like postage stamps and bookplates, and in small finely-carved sculpture. Artists such as William Blake, Samuel Palmer, John Linnell, Edward Calvert, George Richmond, Charles Ricketts and Edward Burne-Jones did not hesitate to express themselves in these arts of *multum in parvo* when they felt it best conveyed their concepts. Miniature art is art expressed with the spirit of the jeweller; it is to large painting what a madrigal is to an oratorio; or, as the Chinese poet Lu Chi put it: 'In a sheet of paper is contained the infinite'. The miniaturist must be able, as William Blake wrote '... to see the World in a Grain of Sand': therein lies the thisness, the inscape of the miniaturist's art. It is by these standards that the miniature arts ought to be judged; like any other art they should be conceived and assessed on their own terms.

Big is not necessarily best: *mega biblion mega kakon* (a big book is a big evil). But both the immense and the diminutive are impressive: one views each with astonishment, wondering how human hands could have wrought either. At one extreme are the Colossi of Thebes, the enormous spatial harmonies of the interior of St Peter's, Michelangelo's tremendous frescoes in the Sistine Chapel; at the other extreme are a penetrating portrait by Hans Holbein, little more than two inches in diameter, a Japanese netsuke group of half a dozen monkeys, all perfectly carved in finest detail, yet overall less than an inch and a half in height, a cameo portrait by Carl Fabergé carved from a tiny slice of nacre. All are awesome, as the ancient Greeks fully appreciated; they honoured their architects and sculptors, but special appreciation was reserved for their celators or engravers of dies for minting coins. One is still astonished at being able to hold between two fingers a tetradrachm by Kimon or Euainetos, a tiny yet powerful masterpiece as compelling as a section of the marble frieze of the Parthenon.

Only when I had straightened out all of this in my mind did I again take up my brushes and begin to paint once more. The world I depicted (and still paint when I can, although my eyes are no longer capable of long periods of sustained concentration) was a realm of moods: of rapturous ecstasy, of pensive sadness, of wistful nostalgia, a world of nocturnes, of visual lyrics, of perceptible Lieder; and occasionally of high spirits. As in my earlier paintings, there were swans – always swans, I could never escape them at this period of my life – ballerinas, nymphs, cypresses, blue mountains, peacocks, flowers, tombs and moons: everything in fact that could be gathered together to express my current moods. My metaphysical, surreal world, my landscapes of dreams suffered no shadow, but all was bathed in a uniform light.

****

For me this was a lonely interval; most of my friends served in the armed forces, and my friends in the ballet had receded into the background. However, on a visit to a young German refugee to whom I was temporarily attracted, I glimpsed a fleeting view of future happiness. I had arrived at her Cambridge flat one summer's evening, bearing one or two recent miniatures, and soon afterwards her flatmate came in accompanied by her young sister and cousin, who had just arrived in Cambridge to take up a post in the University. All three exclaimed in admiration seeing my work, but my own attention was wholly absorbed by the strikingly beautiful cousin. She was very young, and I was a mature twenty-five, so I firmly put aside any idea of making advances. Yet I departed dreaming and three years later we fell in love and married, but more of that later.

Eight
Re-Embarkation

I returned to Cambridge in September 1945 soon after the end of the War, and began at once to take up slackness that had crept into the family business, owing largely to dubious office management. Despite my father's great business acumen, he suffered from incurably poor eyesight, which prevented him from delving very deeply into the state of the firm's bookkeeping. I therefore made this my prime task, and quite soon had everything under firm control.

Having straightened out our books and accounts, I set about re-laying the foundations of our architectural metalworking workshop. I saw that there would be much reconstruction and rebuilding when the ravages of bombing and, hardly less, those of wartime neglect, were made good. We should try to get our share of new work, but I found the conservation and restoration of antique ironwork especially attractive. Much had been swept away for possible use in munitions, but most of it was never used and lay rusting in corporation dumps, a typical example of wartime philistinism. So what had been allowed to remain should be conserved, and its survival ensured. We employed some of the most skilful blacksmiths in England, to whose impeccable skill such work could confidently be entrusted: several of them later received awards for this from the City of London's Worshipful Company of Blacksmiths.

Some of the finest architectural ironwork in the country was conserved in our workshops, from the garden arbour, popularly known as 'The Birdcage', at Melbourne Hall in Derbyshire, made by the great smith Robert Bakewell in about 1708-11, to the magnificent 19th-century cast iron and wrought iron aviary at Waddesdon in Buckinghamshire.

Repairs made before our conservation were often quite horrifying: in some cases whole areas of scrollwork had been replaced by third-rate modern copies electrically welded into position. When the 'Birdcage' came into our workshops, my father believed it beyond repair and was tremendously worried lest I should have submitted an estimate for an impossible task. But he need not have worried, for the 'Birdcage' now stands in its original position at Melbourne, with its slender and sensitive outlines as fresh, as elegant as when it left Robert Bakewell's forge.

In addition to restoration and conservation work, we made much new work, including numerous items connected with the rebuilding of the badly blitzed centre of Coventry, designed by the City Architect, Arthur Ling. They included the enormous coat of arms in beaten copper on the Belgrade Theatre, the framework and faces on the clock above the retail market, and the cast iron and mild steel balustrading in the pedestrian shopping precinct. For the Master's Lodge at St. John's College, Cambridge, we made a pair of wrought iron entrance gates, designed by David Roberts, with a beautiful interlacing monogram, designed by Reynolds Stone, of the initials of the Master and his wife: JGMW, Sir James and Lady [Gertrude] Mann Wordie. For Sir Nikolaus Pevsner we made a pair of churchyard gates, to be erected in memory of his wife. Incidentally, I did not take to Pevsner, whom I found decidedly humourless and dogmatic; nor for that matter do I consider him a good architectural historian, for his work is vitiated by carelessness and inaccuracy. Yet it is fashionable to express breathless admiration of his industry, and no doubt it will take a little time for the truth to emerge.

A commission which did not materialise was to have been for entrance gates for Christopher Hassall's 12th-century fortified house, Tolford Manor, near Canterbury. Christopher suffered an horrendous heart attack and died in April 1963 on a train journey. His friend, Geoffrey Keynes, said he might have been saved if he could have been taken from the train for immediate attention, but, sad to relate, it was not to be; among the minor consequences of his death was the abandonment of the gates.

For the first Lord Fairhaven we made a wrought iron and repoussé table, designed by me, with his arms among the decorations. Its top, and the *raison d'être* of the piece, is a large mosaic panel of tiny tesserae of the type and size usually reserved for jewellery and small Italian views: it was one of the largest extant examples of its kind (Fairhaven liked to have the largest things: in his Anglesey Abbey garden is the largest porphyry urn in the world). We also made for him a wrought iron sign to be awarded each year for the Best Kept Village in Cambridgeshire. I made what I considered to be a pleasant modern design, but Fairhaven would not look at it, insisting on an Italianate concoction with vine leaves and luxuriant bunches of grapes. Well, he was paying for it, and we made what he wanted, but it is not one of my favourite examples of blacksmithery.

I found Lord Fairhaven a strange man, impossibly shy and selfconscious, and absurdly formal beyond imagination, deporting himself like a grand seigneur of an earlier age. He rarely asked a direct question, but made his factotum do it for him. I noticed one day that he continually eyed a new cavalry-twill jacket I was wearing – a distinctly cut country garment with leather buttons, a longer-than-usual skirt, and buttoned bellows pockets. On my next visit to the Abbey, his man waylaid me as I was approaching the front door. 'Excuse me, Mr. Lister', he said, 'Would you mind telling me who is your tailor?' 'Not at all, Pratt Manning of Cambridge.' I already knew that Fairhaven had his suits made at the same firm, for Mr. Rowe the cutter had told me so. Following this, his lordship became progressively more distant, no doubt believing it 'side' on the part of a blacksmith to use the same tailor as himself. Finally, instead of discussing work with me, he preferred to deal with one of my craftsmen, who addressed almost every sentence to him preceded by the words 'My Lord', which Fairhaven obviously enjoyed.

His collection, which may still be seen at Anglesey Abbey during the summer months, is enormous and eclectic, and ranges from mediaeval German limewood sculpture to bijouterie and silver plate, from Gothic tapestries to paintings by William Etty, Alfred Munnings and Edwin Landseer to mention only a segment. He undoubtedly had a strong Royalty fixation, for the largest room in the Abbey is full of views of Windsor Castle, though not far away are the two great Altieri Claudes, formerly the property of Marina, Duchess of Kent, which artistically are worth more than all the rest of the collection lumped together. The atmosphere is all somewhat suffocating high camp, but colourful and not unoriginal, despite overtones of parvenu wealth.

I am sorry to say that the family firm no longer employs blacksmiths. Few boys in recent years have wanted to take up apprenticeships in this trade, and we therefore found it difficult to keep an adequate staff together. Also, from the mid 'seventies and the onset of high inflation, fewer and fewer patrons have been willing or able to afford to commission good work. Inflation also brought much higher overhead costs, which meant that the hourly rates put the price of decorative wrought ironwork beyond the purse of all but a very few. Such considerations in 1978 forced on the Lister firm the closure of its long-established blacksmiths' shop, with its honourable tradition of fine craftsmanship, and the whole effort of our workshops was channelled into rather boring machine and sheet-metal work – boring at any rate to me. Such decisions were forced for the same reasons on many similar firms in other parts of England.

Many blacksmiths do flourish in this country, but almost invariably they are in small establishments with few overheads, employing at most two or three craftsmen. Some of these men are doing work which may be compared with the best ironwork from the past. May they continue to 'flourish root and branch!'

****

I did not neglect my painting during this period. My work began to attract recognition from critics and professional miniaturists, and in 1946 I was elected a member of the Royal Society of Miniature Painters. I remained in the Society for many years, and served as its President for ten years until 1980, when I resigned. I ought to have resigned much earlier, for I found its policies contrary to almost everything I believe in and stand for in painting; ninety per cent of the works in its exhibitions seemed to me to show little awareness of any post-Victorian artistic development. The miniaturists' mentors were Alma-Tadema, Leighton, W.P. Frith, Augustus Egg and their compeers, far greater artists than themselves, who had already said everything there was to say in their credo.

There were, despite this, a few very good miniaturists, the best of all being Joan Ayling and Lisa de Montfort whose portraiture has an elegance reminiscent of the work of Rex Whistler. But try as I might (and I wrote a couple of books and a succession of articles, and arranged a few general exhibitions of miniatures in London and the provinces) I could never succeed in persuading the vast majority of miniaturists to look beyond their tightly executed, crudely coloured snapshot-like confections. If only they had returned to the fount of their art and studied Nicholas Hilliard's *Treatise concerning the Arte of Limning* (1624; first published 1912), if only they had studied the works of great miniaturists, if only they had built on these traditions and developed them, the miniature might have become one of the most acclaimed forms of visual art in the 20th century. For its very diminutiveness, its very intimacy would have accorded well with the restrictions of modern living accommodation. Large pictures, whether landscapes, portraits or what you will, seem overpowering in the small rooms of modern flats, villas and cottages, while many miniatures may be accommodated either on the walls or in cabinets, but nobody will buy or commission them if they are unimaginative, boring, ill-conceived and maladroitly executed.

Miniaturists simply did not respond to my encouragement and blandishment, and few were prepared even to try. What was needed in the portrait miniature was the *poudre de riz* and rouge elegance of a Marie Laurencin, a Tamara de Lempicka or an Erté, expressed in the techniques and materials of miniature, maintaining the essence of the art within a new vision. The fact remains that no new Cosway or Engleheart emerged to leave to posterity a miniaturist's interpretation of 20th-century society.

Artistically acceptable miniatures of other subjects are even fewer; their last great exponents were Victorian or post-Victorian artists, such as William Morris, Florence

Kingsford, wife of Sir Sydney Cockerell, and my own mentor, Albert Cousins, who, like mediaeval *historieurs*, used subject miniatures to decorate illuminated manuscripts; and, though he is a bright exception, there is the work of the little-known yet vital watercolourist and poet, Russell George Alexander, who painted intense jewel-like and tiny landscapes that could hardly have been conceived before the 20th century.

There is little more to show; yet some painters of larger works could have suggested the way in which such miniatures could develop, such as the *animalier* Franz Marc, who combined vivid colour with metallic leaf; Marc Chagall, painter of vibrant multi-coloured dreams; Max Ernst, who worked with encrusted, almost jewelled textures; René Magritte, who used exquisite textures to convey his surrealist visions; and nearer home, and best of all, the poet-artist David Jones, whose fine, closely-textured and minutely-wrought water-colours, while essentially modern, are reminiscent of landscapes in the missals and horae of Northern Europe in the 15th century. There are dozens of such artists who might have provided examples of points of departure for the 20th-century miniaturist, who could have suggested a way of looking at things to kindle a vigorous vision, achieving a special insight into the contemporary world. Few have accepted the challenge.

Nine
Marriage

*

The supreme event in my life and its most important pivotal point happened some months after my return to Cambridge: my marriage. Rather impulsively I became betrothed to a young lady whom I had known for some time, the daughter of a Cambridgeshire farmer. It became apparent after an interval of little more than a couple of months that the engagement was a complete disaster. Breaking point came one evening after I had taken my fiancée to a presentation of Chekhov's *Cherry Orchard* in the A.D.C. Theatre. To my delighted surprise, the part of Anya, daughter of Madame Ranevsky, was taken by the young girl I had met at the flat of my German refugee friend three years previously. She was now an exquisitely lovely young lady of twenty, and it was crystal clear to me that here was the love of my life. I had not previously taken in her name, but here it was in the programme, in capitals: PAMELA BRUTNELL.

Within twenty-four hours my earlier engagement was terminated by mutual consent, and a letter was on its way to Pamela, asking her if she would dine with me a few days later. We began happily and have continued happily ever since, and although, as I write this, we are grandparents, we have never lost our delight in one another, have never lost our initial love. We have an harmonious sense of humour, appreciate each other's tastes in art, literature and music, and even coincide in many of them, and if we disagree, as is sometimes inevitable, it is with good humour and mutual understanding. This may sound too good to be true: I can only state the fact and say that I would not change a thing. Love is almost indefinably concealed from those ill-fated souls unpenetrated by the arrows of Eros, so I will merely observe that it changed my life for the better in every way.

Some eighteen months later, on June 7, 1947, we were married by Sam Senior at Pamela's Cambridge church, Holy Trinity. There was a somewhat ecumenical element in the event, for my bride's present to me was a superb illuminated manuscript by Albert Cousins, of the Catholic service of Benediction of the Blessed Sacrament, which she had commissioned, and had bound by Sandy Cockerell of Letchworth.

My parents delighted in my choice and from the beginning treated Pamela as the daughter they had never had, but passionately would have liked. My father sometimes spoke eloquently to me about my good fortune in finding such a spouse, but between my mother and Pamela a very special relationship flourished; they were completely devoted to one another, so much so that their mutual understanding could hardly have been deeper. They never exchanged cross words, and surprisingly the same was true of my father: Pamela must have been the only person who knew him who could say that!

We set up home in an ancient and pretty thatched cottage, Low Thatch, in the attractive South Cambridgeshire village of West Wratting. Here we settled in idyllic happiness; here I could spread my books (on miniature painting, ballet and fine printing) around the walls, to say nothing of Pamela's, mostly poetry from Chaucer to our own day, and editions of Jane Austen. We made a herb garden in a corner overlooking a meadow, from which inquisitive bullocks would gaze intently at us across the hedge. We installed a cote stocked with pigeons which I am sorry to say disappeared within a month or so, shot I feared by locals who objected to raids on their new peas.

We had no electricity, for it did not come to the village until eighteen months after we had moved in, so we relied on oil lamps and candles for illumination, and an oil stove for cooking: it took an hour to boil a kettle on this. Despite such inconveniences (but were they really inconvenient?), it was very romantic, on an autumn or winter evening, to sit near the log fire in the inglenook, eating delicious black-crusted bread from the local bakery with local honey, or reading by candlelight, to the accompaniment of dancing shadows thrown by the fire and the candles on the whitewashed walls.

In 1947 West Wratting remained a rural retreat, almost cut off from the modern world; with petrol rationing in force, casual motoring was impossible, few people in the village had a telephone and not many owned a wireless set. Few of the locals did their shopping in the nearby towns of Newmarket, Cambridge or Saffron Walden, although we enjoyed an intermittent if somewhat unreliable bus service to Cambridge. The village store, with its delicious compound aroma of cheese, leather, paraffin, tea, bacon, bread and fruit, supplied us with our every need: it stocked even ready-made haberdashery.

Characters abounded, among whom was Billy Rash (incredibly married to a Miss Itch), the village chimney sweep and general odd-job man. He worked at sundry times for Miss Younghusband, an elderly spinster who, anxious to promote his education, presented him with her discarded women's periodicals, but mindful of his reputation as a rustic philanderer, carefully clipped out all advertisements for women's underwear before handing them over. A more respectable character, Sid Roope, combined the callings of cobbler, barber, postman and apiarist (he constructed the hives himself). Sid's much less industrious brother Joe occasionally dug our garden. My first encounter with him was on the evening we arrived home from our honeymoon: I answered a knock on the back door to discover Joe, touching his cap and announcing, 'I'm just a-going to the pub to 'ave a drink along o' the wedding o' yourn!' Who could resist that? He left, happily clutching a couple of pieces of silver, which he doubtless quickly transformed into beer.

I asked Joe to demolish an old brick privy in the garden, with a metal bucket under the seat, as we had installed a modern water-closet in the cottage. Having carried out this task, Joe asked, 'Can I 'ave they old bucket?'

'Do what you like with it', I said.

'Ah,' said Joe, 'I'll clean he an' make a bob o' he up the village!'

The mind boggles at the thought of some unfortunate village

householder transporting his water from the village pump in this utensil.

Joe was a philosopher. He gave not a fig for the modern world. 'I've never seen a railway, an' don't want,' he said, and added: 'I've never been out of the parish, an' don't want.' I found it difficult to believe this, but on enquiry his claims were confirmed. How happier would be the lot of those who consider themselves his betters if they enjoyed equal content!

The Women's Institute provided many blithe episodes. For a prize offered at one meeting for the best fish mousse, the members put their best creative efforts into making the creamiest, most succulent mousses they could devise, and then put them outside on the steps of the village hall to cool and set, only to discover when they were ready to bring them inside for judging, that the village dogs had been there first and had licked out each bowl as clean as if it had been washed. When a Women's Institute outing to London was arranged, Billy Rash decided to go with it. As the only man in the party, he had no wish to embarrass the ladies by stopping the coach so that he could make water, so he abstained from all liquids for a full forty-eight hours before the party's departure. Nobody could have accused Billy of being deficient in gallantry.

We remained at Low Thatch for three years, after which we began to find the accommodation restricting, especially as we wanted to start a family. So we decided to move, and I put the sale of the cottage into the hands of an estate agent, who rather grandly advertised it, with a photograph, in *Country Life* and, more realistically, in the local press. All to no avail, for he produced hardly a viewer, let alone a buyer. I then decided I would try to sell it myself, and was much luckier, for within twenty-four hours of my discreet advertisement appearing in the *Cambridge Daily News*, I received a letter from a Mrs Anna Gosse, in which she said that Low Thatch seemed to be just what she was looking for. She came out post-haste on the bus, declared herself enchanted and telephoned her husband to come out at once by taxi to see if he agreed.

He turned out to be Philip Gosse who, I afterwards learned, was a doctor of medicine, author of a standard history of piracy, a splendid essayist, and *inter alia*, the son of Sir Edmund Gosse, sometime Librarian of the House of Lords, chief literary critic on *The Sunday Times*, and author of the classic autobiographical study *Father and Son* (1907). We later learned that Mrs. Gosse was the poet and novelist Anna Gordon Keown and sister of Eric Keown, the dramatic critic of *Punch*. The Gosses bought Low Thatch without hesitation, which was a great relief to us. But, more important, their visit began a deep and happy friendship, which only ceased when they died.

As for Pamela and me, we moved temporarily into a flat in the centre of Cambridge, which tided us over until we found new permanent quarters suitable for accommodating a family. This came eventually in 1951 in the form of another, but larger thatched cottage, Cockertons, on the outskirts of the village of Linton, a few miles south-west of West Wratting.

Ten
Philip Gosse and Friends

During the next few years Philip Gosse became one of our closest friends. Deeply interested in everything I did, he encouraged me in everything I attempted, and introduced me to many people in the mainstream of the literary establishment.

He was an impressive character, not very tall, but with a thick-set, broad-shouldered body and an almost Napoleonic stance; his great head was surmounted with a mane of greying red hair. His long face had a strong chin, and his upper lip was decorated by a bristling military moustache; his bright, wickedly twinkling eyes were crested with long, beetling eyebrows, like untidy straw thatch. He moved with the rolling gait of a sailor (not inappropriate in one who was an authority on piracy): this, together with his general appearance, gave him a distinctly aggressive air: one, I hasten to add, that completely belied his almost innocent good nature. Not that he was in every way gentle: he had a schoolboyish love of practical jokes; he betrayed a strong seam of insensitivity in his banter; if anybody wanted a row, he could meet him more than halfway; and he attacked all forms of injustice wherever he saw them. But nobody forgave more quickly, he was generous to a fault and ferociously loyal to his many friends.

Anna – gentle, fey, poetic Anna – was Philip's third wife and a perfect partner. They met in unpromising circumstances: she was staying at a Cambridge hotel when she found that her ears needed syringing. The hotel manager recommended a local doctor and Anna duly presented herself at his surgery, to find a Dr Philip Gosse acting in locum tenens. He syringed her ears and cleared them, but only after he had drenched her to the skin in the process. Anna returned to the hotel, complaining loudly about the 'terrible Dr Gosse' who had caused her to make a complete change of clothing. Notwithstanding this, three weeks later she had to admit that the same Dr Gosse, whom she had met again several times since, had asked her to marry him, and she had accepted.

Although, or probably because, Anna seemed the opposite to Philip in almost every way, they made an ideal pair, firstly I think because they shared so many interests, but secondly and probably more importantly, because they shared a keen sense of the ridiculous and spent much of their time laughing helplessly at the oddities of the world. When they stayed in hotels, people looked at them with raised eyebrows, for their conversation during meals was so animated that they appeared to be lover and mistress rather than husband and wife. Not the least of their amusement came from the situations they brought upon themselves through ingenuous misunderstandings. Typical of these was the occasion when Philip, in the middle of the night, and clothed only in his pyjamas, got himself locked in the lavatory. His angry cries brought Anna running to the landing.

'For God's sake get me out,' he shouted, 'I'm frozen!' But release him she could not, and having held up his dressing gown on the end of a cobweb brush outside the lavatory window, from which his arm shot forth and angrily snatched it, Anna hurried off to telephone Mr Roberts the plumber. A sleepy though cultured voice answered.

'Is that Mrs Roberts?' asked Anna.

'Yes'.

'Then you must tell your husband to come immediately. Dr Gosse is locked in the lavatory.'

This was received by what can only be described as a startled pause, followed by the bewildered comment, 'I don't *really* understand what my husband can do to help. He is the Vice-Chancellor of the University.' Anna in her excitement had dialled by mistake the number of their friend, S.C. Roberts, Master of Pembroke College.

Philip and Anna once met a couple whom they began to like so much that they arranged to go on holiday with them to Switzerland. But not long after planning this, they began to find their new friends distinctly irritating, and made their excuses, saying that they had after all to stay in Cambridge due to pressure of work. Having, as they thought, tactfully saved the day, they took themselves off for a holiday in Stresa. On arrival they settled in their hotel room, unpacked their luggage, and Philip threw open the french doors which led on to a balcony overlooking the lake. He took in the splendid view, with Isola Bella, like a marmoreal galleon, floating in the distance when, looking to his left, he descried the couple whom they had sought to avoid, sunning themselves on the next balcony. He never told me how he and Anna had extricated themselves from the embarrassing situation.

Philip matriculated at Cambridge when sixty-five – surely a record – and Trinity College accepted him as a Fellow Commoner. At Trinity he often caused staid dons to blush, as when one evening during dinner at high table he was seated opposite a distinguished American Democrat politician, whom he startled during dessert by pulling open his jacket and displaying a tie embroidered with the sentiment: I LIKE IKE.

Even the Gosses' servants were eccentric. A daily help whom Philip called 'The Female Impersonator' resembled Clarkson Rose in the part of Widow Twankey in *Aladdin*. Another, an Irish maid, spent her spare time reading the life of Christ to the cat; many were the times Anna went into the kitchen to hear such phrases as 'And Jesus went down to Capernaum' being shouted in a broad Irish brogue into the cat's ear. During her working hours this daughter of Erin spent most of her time polishing the front windows, so that she could wave to her boyfriend who drove a bus on that route.

Philip's cat, 'Ninny', was a character akin in many ways to Thomas Hardy's dog 'Wessex'. After the end of World War II, during one of the frequent Cold War crises, there was some talk of reviving the Home Guard and registration forms were circulated. This gave Philip an irresistible opportunity for one of his pranks, and he submitted a form for the cat, in which he stated that Ninian Gosse wanted to be a Home Guardsman. To the question 'What was your wartime occupation?' Philip, answered, 'Fire-watching.' What he had not expected was a visit from an earnest young recruiting officer, asking if he might speak to Mr Ninian Gosse. Philip's resourcefulness was not exhausted: putting his finger to his lips he whispered, 'Ssh! There has been a death in the family. Not a word to Mrs Gosse – it would upset her.' The officer's sympathy overflowed, and he was invited in to drink a glass of sherry, during which time, in the words of Philip, 'his eyes already close together, got closer and closer – from grief.'

Philip knew all his literary contemporaries and many of those of his father. He was a marvellous raconteur and delighted Pamela and me with feasts of anecdote. He spoke, for instance, of the poet J.C. Squire, who was a notorious alcoholic. Philip told us how a titled lady took pity on him, and seeking to cure him, suggested that he should spend a few months at her stately home, on condition that while there he should eschew all alcoholic liquor. Squire accepted with alacrity as he was, as usual, penniless. However, things did not work out as his noble hostess planned, for by the time her guest returned home, she was as confirmed an inebriate as he.

In 1935, after Squire had been knighted, the artist Ernest Proctor, one of Philip's friends, wrote this witty effusion:

Good day, Sir Jack,
– a dizzy flight
First Knave, then Squire
And now Good Knight.

With several other poems from his distinguished visitors, Philip had this printed in an edition of twenty-five copies, each poem, the title page and colophon, on a separate leaf, and issued them from his Sussex home, Weppons, below Chanctonbury Ring, under the title *Weppons of Peace*. There were contributions from A.J.A. Symons, Clifford Bax, Arthur Waugh, Vyvyan Holland and others. Philip gave me a set inscribed, 'For my one and only collector'; that set and his own are the only ones I have ever seen.

Of Max Beerbohm, Philip said he never answered letters. He

had the manuscript of a sonnet written by his father and Max, each writing a line and sending it to the other to add the next one. When Evan Charteris was writing his *Life and Letters of Sir Edmund Gosse* (1921), Philip sent circular letters to former acquaintances and friends of his father, asking for recollections of him. Among the replies was a folio letter from Bernard Shaw (instead of Shaw's usual postcard) describing how Edmund Gosse had introduced Shaw to (of all people) Rudyard Kipling, at Thomas Hardy's funeral. Much to Philip's chagrin, Charteris, who was noted for carelessness, lost this letter. To appease him, Charteris gave him the manuscript of the Gosse/Beerbohm sonnet; Philip later discovered that Max had lent it to Charteris in connection with the same work. He said he did not return it because anyway Max would not acknowledge it.

The Waughs were related to the Gosses. Philip told me that when Evelyn was an unknown writer he used to put the dust jacket of his own latest book around the one he was carrying, and hold it up with some ostentation while reading it on the bus or the tube. Of Coventry Patmore, Philip said he had a son named Epiphany, who was called 'Piffy' by his school friends. He told me also that when he was at Haileybury there was a boy who answered to the nickname of 'Don't tread in it'. This lad had a photograph of his fifteen-year old sister in the nude, and boys were allowed to look at it for threepence a time. At the end of the Great War he was created a baronet for making a fortune from munitions.

I once sold to Hubert David, the bookseller, a number of books I no longer wanted, and among them was Robert Louis Stevenson's *Memories and Portraits* (1887). Philip saw it on David's bookstall and espied my bookplate inside. He bought it and returned it to me after adding the inscription: 'Found on David's bookstall and returned to the Lister library by one who was a friend, though a young one, of R.L.S.' As for bookstalls, Philip sometimes amused himself if one of his own books happened to be on sale, by taking it up while the stallholder was otherwise occupied, and inscribing it: 'To G.K. Chesterton from the author', chuckling over an unsuspecting collector of Chestertoniana acquiring it as a prized association copy.

Philip's practice as a doctor was as haphazard as the other

segments of his life. His father had been insistent that he should have a profession, and the choice fell unwisely on medicine. For Philip, on his own admission, must have been the world's worst doctor, despite having been, for a brief period in later life, head of the Radium Institute. I once asked him if he knew Mr. Victor Rolfe, a well-known Cambridge pharmacist. 'Yes' he said, 'he is a great friend of mine, and has saved me trouble with my prescriptions on several occasions. He telephoned me only last week to ask if I intended the 500 grains of strychnine phosphate to mean .005 grain.' And there was the wartime story of the W.A.A.F. private with a swollen abdomen who was taken by her mother to be examined by Philip, who diagnosed wind and prescribed soda mints. Six weeks later she gave birth to a bonny son.

Philip's sister, the talented painter Sylvia Gosse, erstwhile pupil of Walter Sickert, appeared occasionally at his house. An exact feminine version of her brother, she could have been Philip in drag; they were so alike both in appearance and personality – almost *Doppelgängers* – that they could never meet without quarrelling. Away from one another, they were the best of friends, exchanging newsy and amiable letters, but as soon as they met, what an explosion! Sylvia's paintings closely resembled those of her mentor, yet they do have an inherent quality, being generally more lightly conceived both in composition and technique. Her greatest originality lay in her etchings, among which is an excellent and well-known study of her father seated at his library desk in his house in Regent's Park.

Every year for Philip's birthday, Pamela made him a special cake, and he looked forward to this with schoolboyish excitement and delight, and I must say that her creations were highly original. The first one celebrated Philip's interest in the history of piracy: on top was a pirate galleon complete with the Jolly Roger, sailing on a sea of blue icing, and around the base were silver- and gold-foil covered chocolate coins to represent pieces of eight. Another year, she put a tiny catapult on the cake, with the legend in icing: 'Philip toujours un gosse.'

Philip was a staunch and fiercely defensive friend. This was forcibly demonstrated to me when the reputation of A.J.A. Symons was being somewhat besmirched by the bibliopole

Percy Muir. Symons (known to his friends as 'A.J.') was the author of the classic *The Quest for Corvo* (1934), which he completed in Philip's garden at Weppons. Symons had many shortcomings, but he was kind-hearted and when, between the Wars, Percy Muir got into financial difficulties, A.J. at once set up a rescue fund and helped to get Percy back on to firm ground. Philip therefore took strong exception when Percy's derogatory remarks were published for, as he said, even if Percy's strictures were true, it ill befitted Percy to utter them. But it did not stop there. Philip wanted everybody, me included, to hate Percy. I had some years before given a snuff-sampling evening at Cockertons and Philip and Percy were among the guests. Later, when Philip had taken a dislike to Percy, he told me that he had received a letter from him, in which he had made fun of me and of my snuff party. 'You can look at it after I have died,' he declared, 'it is in my copy of *Books at Bedtime*' (a small book we had compiled together in 1953). I did, out of curiosity, look for it after Philip died, as one of his executors, but it was not there. I did not believe then that it existed and as time passed and I got to know Percy better, I am sure Philip had imagined it.

Philip Gosse introduced me, early in our friendship, to another bibliophile and scholar, who was to remain a lifelong friend: Geoffrey Keynes. This happened when Pamela and I, and Arthur Astbury, who was on one of his weekend visits, were invited by Anna to tea at West Wratting. This proved a typical muddled Gosse entertainment, everybody drinking somebody else's tea, with teacakes, buns and bread and butter being handed round, all in the wrong order; at one stage Anna staggered into the room with an enormous pottery bowl, at the bottom of which were four forlorn-looking and burnt scones. In truth it resembled the Mad Tea Party in *Alice's Adventures in Wonderland*. Geoffrey Keynes and his wife Margaret (née Darwin) were very genial. Geoffrey looked about fifteen years younger than his age, exceedingly well groomed, and could easily have been mistaken for a retired army officer. We enjoyed much talk of Siegfried Sassoon and Rupert Brooke between Philip and Geoffrey, and later Philip produced a photograph of himself as a little boy, wrapped in Robert Louis Stevenson's shawl; probably this childhood friendship with the author of *Treasure Island* first implanted in Philip's heart his love of piracy and pirates.

Soon after this, Margaret Keynes wrote, inviting me to tea at Lammas House, Brinkley, their home, to view her family silhouette portraits. Both Geoffrey and herself received me most cordially: they wanted to know everything about Pamela and Rory, our new son, and seemed most interested in all our doings. All in all, these teas at West Wratting and Brinkley marked the beginning of a deep and genial friendship both for Pamela and me.

I already knew something of Geoffrey's library and Blake collection, and when on my next visit he showed me some of his treasures, I was amazed by the breadth of his collecting interests: Jane Austen, John Keats, Robert Boyle, William Harvey, John Donne, these represent but a tithe of them: Philip had well-named him 'The Jackdaw'. His books stood two deep on his bookshelves, many of them in fine modern bindings (he was incidentally a shareholder in Dickie Band's firm, John P. Gray and Son Ltd, the craft bookbinders). Staffordshire zebras were massed – one might with accuracy call them a herd – on top of his bookcases.

It would be impossible for anybody, however rich, to amass such a library today. For one thing the material is just not available, for another prices have become prohibitive even if it were. Geoffrey began to collect before the Great War, when rare and fine books could be had for the proverbial 'old song'. More than once when visiting us, I have shown him a recent acquisition. 'How much did you have to pay for it?' was his invariable question. I would tell him – it may perhaps have been £100 or £150 – and he would say with a chuckle, 'I bought mine in 1914 for half-a-crown!' He was a predatory collector – how many collectors are not? I once asked him if he saw for sale an impression of the card William Blake engraved for George Cumberland, would he let me know? It is an attractive small engraving which encapsulates within a few square inches much that is typical of Blake's vision, and I have always wanted to possess it, though it has never come my way, 'Yes,' said Geoffrey, 'I will let you know: I have five.'

In this he reminded me somewhat of Philip's American friend John S. Mayfield, a well-known Swinburne scholar and collector. There was a rare Swinburne booklet, which had been issued in a certified limited edition of one hundred and fifty copies, and Mayfield set himself the task of tracing, and if possible acquiring, every copy. He succeeded, but much to his chagrin discovered there were one hundred and fifty-five copies in circulation.

Yet Geoffrey's bibliographical taste fell short of the omnivorous, as he indicated when Philip sought to present him with Sappho's poems, printed in an edition limited to *one* copy for presentation to his father, beautifully bound by Rivière in richly tooled morocco, with silk *doublures* and with goffered and gilded edges. 'I wonder', said Philip, 'if you would accept this for your library'.

'No, thank you', said Geoffrey without hesitation, handing the treasure back to a crestfallen Philip.

This may sound rudely ungracious to those who did not know him. But it was not that, Geoffrey simply did not want the book and would have considered it dishonest to have accepted it and deprived Philip of it through mere politeness. He was indeed transparently honest. And he lacked pomposity. One evening he was my guest at a dinner in Cambridge and had on his other side my friend Jack King, who was at that time Bursar of Wolfson College. Geoffrey asked Jack what he did. 'I am a bursar', said Jack. 'I had a brother who was a bursar' rejoined Geoffrey, which, when one thinks about it, was a startling understatement of the profession of John Maynard Keynes, even if he was once Bursar of King's College.

I never met Maynard, for he died just before I met Geoffrey. But I often saw him, with his wonderful little wife, Lydia Lopokova the ballerina, for they had a *pied à terre* in St. Edward's Passage, over David's bookshop. She was the least glamorous of women, never used make up, nor wore smart clothes, and thought nothing of walking about in an ageing mackintosh, and a headscarf, and perhaps carrying a bucket or broom she had just bought. Dickie Band told me the Maynard Keyneses regularly visited his bindery. Maynard would walk in, followed by Lydia carrying a heavy pile of books as if she were a porter, no doubt thinking of her husband's weak heart.

Geoffrey had many amusing recollections of his brother, none more so than that which he mentioned when he was dining with me in hall at my college. Seated opposite to him was a noted lady philosopher who told him she had just been reading Maynard's *Treatise of Probability* (1921).

'Did you understand it?' he asked.

'Yes, perfectly.'

'Strange', said Geoffrey, 'my brother could not understand it himself when he tried to read it some years after it came out.'

Eleven
Publishing and Book Making

During the early 1950s I began in a small way to publish books. I felt that there might be a market for books on unfamiliar or unfashionable subjects, well-produced and issued in limited editions. World War II had forced utility standards on book producers, which led to everything from paper to binding being third rate. There remained nothing comparable with the books of the Nonesuch, Golden Cockerel, St Dominic's and other private presses of the 1920s and 1930s. And, despite cheaper standards of production, it became practically impossible to get a work into print if its subject was so specialised as to limit its sales potential to a hundred or so copies. It seemed to me (without attempting to emulate those of Nonesuch and its peers), that with careful budgeting and reasonably high standards, it might be possible to fill at least part of the vacuum, so I decided, soon after we had moved to Linton, to publish one or two small books by way of experiment.

I knew an excellent printer in Cambridge, P.A. Parfitt, who during the 1920s and 1930s had produced the *Festival Theatre Review* for Terence Gray. He readily agreed to help me, and as an experiment he printed in 1952, in an edition of sixty copies, a small card-cased booklet compiled by myself called *A Title List of Books on Miniature Painting*, a short introduction to literature on this art; it sold out within a week or two of its publication. Thus encouraged I proceeded, between 1952 and 1954, to publish five further books.

Of these one was especially attractive to me. I had for some years toyed with the idea of writing a book on Léon Bakst, Diaghilev's finest designer. At the time his work was somewhat unfashionable, his designs could sometimes be bought for as little as £150, and I could find no publisher willing to take the risk of commissioning such a book. I therefore decided to write and publish a small illustrated monograph, with one plate hand-coloured by Pamela and me and several black and white plates, somewhat more limited in scope than what I had originally envisaged. For all that, I still consider that *The Muscovite Peacock* (1954) is not a bad introduction to Bakst's work.

In researching for this essay, I consulted many who had known Bakst. I even wrote to galleries in Leningrad and Moscow (difficult in those days to contact) and received many photographs and much information through the Soviet Embassy in London ... six months after the book was published. By far the most helpful of my correspondents was the Russo-American artist and designer, Simon Lissim, a former pupil of Bakst, who had been a central figure among Russian exiles in Paris before World War II. He had worked during the 1920s on the *émigré* periodical *Jar Ptitza (The Firebird)*. Considerable help was forthcoming also from Pierre Tugal, Curator of *Les Archives Internationales de la Danse* in Paris (now divided between Le Musée de l'Opéra, Paris, and the Dance Museum at the Opera House, Stockholm). I much enjoyed corresponding with Tugal, whose pointed Gallic wit was a joy to read: when I asked him if he could obtain certain information for me, he said nothing would be easier, and he would consult the former Diaghilev dancer, Madame Maria Kuznetsova, and Diaghilev's friend Alexandre Benois. 'For Madame Kuznetsova we must supply a bouquet of flowers or a box of chocolates. For Benois, in view of his age (83) one must hurry'.

I produced two further books before I embarked on more extensive publishing, one of which was *Who's Who in Heaven* by Clifford Bax (1954), a lighthearted piece of froth in blank verse in which the *dramatis personae* are Samuel Pepys, Phryne and Lizzie Siddall. Philip Gosse had put me in touch with Bax, who readily agreed that I might publish his sketch. He lived in a flat in Albany, where I visited him, the first time I had entered that cool and civilised oasis off Piccadilly, with its covered walk, flanked by formal gardens. It was an experience akin to Alice's when she at last penetrated into those cool gardens in Wonderland, after her earlier claustrophobic traumas.

The door was opened by a charming lady, obviously one of Mr Bax's many female friends. She ushered me into the drawing-room and introduced me formally to the old playwright, who sat in his armchair, his feet on a stool, smoking a fragrant cigar and drinking what I later learned was gin and ginger ale. His hands were swollen and distorted by the effects of arthritis, which caused me a pang of conscience when I remembered he had agreed to sign all 250 copies of the edition. His deeply lined face retained something of youth, no doubt because of his sparkling, light blue eyes. A pointed white beard and thinning hair added something of a Chinese sage to his appearance.

He introduced me to another elderly man smoking and drinking with him, a tall, lean, sun-tanned man of upright bearing, dressed in a fawn suit, and wearing a gold-rimmed monocle on a black ribbon. 'This', said Bax, 'is Captain C.B. Fry'. It was indeed the grand old sportsman. 'Mr Bax tells me you are a fine illustrator', he said. This puzzled me as I had never, up to that time, illustrated a book. Perhaps, I suggested, he was thinking of my miniatures. I shall never know what he was thinking of, for Bax broke in at that point, indicating two miniatures, one of himself and one of Meum Stewart. 'These are two very fine miniatures', he said. Indeed they were, for they were painted by my friend, the brilliant miniaturist Lisa de Montfort, and that of Miss Stewart had been reproduced in my book *The British Miniature* (1951).

There was also a romanticised Italian portrait of Shakespeare above the fireplace. Bax said it was labelled on the reverse, 'Signor Guglielmo Shakespeari'. 'It is', he said, 'at least in the true tradition of misrepresentation, in showing the poet with a quill pen raised ready to inscribe some profound observation in a folio volume – no poet ever composed like that'. At this point Fry asked Bax who was his pet poetic aversion: 'T.S. Eliot' he replied unhesitatingly.

Fry talked unceasingly, relating his experiences in Africa, India, at Repton, at Oxford; he quoted some of the Greek lines he had to declaim when, as an undergraduate, he acted in a performance of *The Frogs* of Aristophanes. Among other things he said he was a founder-member of the Royal Automobile Club, and that years ago he sometimes wrote boys' stories in partnership with P.G. Wodehouse. The recollections of this most agreeable raconteur continued throughout the drive I offered him back to his home near Finchley Road.

When, next day, I told Philip about this meeting, he told me that when he was at Haileybury, the games master had lined up the boys along a passage, and stepped out the length of Fry's long-jump record: 23 feet 6 inches. He presented me with one of Clifford Bax's visiting cards on which Clifford had written a verse celebrating an earlier event in which a Mrs Pearson had broken one of his garden hedges by falling into it, and its sequel:

> Like the red flowers that in the meadows bud
> To tell the story of Adonis' blood
> Behold the box-hedge here, ye pious folk,
> That Mrs Pearson's thundering buttocks broke
> And how new snowdrops, fairy branch on branch,
> Commemorate that human avalanche.

Who's Who in Heaven was well received, and it seemed that my publishing idea might prosper. I had published some nicely-produced books, the sales had been encouraging, and I had covered my expenses, even though there was no profit, which had not in any case been my principal consideration. I therefore decided to put everything on a more businesslike foundation as a limited company to be known as the Golden Head Press Ltd. Philip readily agreed to be its chairman, Arthur Astbury its secretary, and my father and brother agreed to become directors and make the same small investment as the others.

Why Golden Head? This name was an offshoot of my work as a miniaturist. I had painted a few silhouette portraits, and until the early years of the nineteenth century, the portrait painter's trade sign was a golden head, and such a sign hung above the door of Cockertons, so I felt it would not be inappropriate to adopt this as the name of our press.

The first book published by the new firm, in 1955, was *A Bibliography of the First Editions of Philip Henry Gosse F.R.S.*, by an old schoolfellow of mine, Peter Stageman, who a little later became Librarian of the Royal Horticultural Society in Vincent Square, London. In passing I should mention that P.H. Gosse was Philip's grandfather, and the father in Sir Edmund Gosse's *Father and Son*. The book contained, in addition to Stageman's bibliography, an essay by Sacheverell Sitwell on Gosse as an illustrator, and another by Geoffrey Lapage, a Cambridge zoologist, on Gosse's work as a scientist. Lapage grumbled because his name was placed after Sitwell's on the title page. Sitwell on the other hand, was both courteous and modest; when the time came to discuss payment, he asked if I thought £15 would be too much, and (this I am sure was meant as kindly encouragement) if I cared to add a copy of my book on Bakst, *The Muscovite Peacock*, it would be very acceptable. I think he let us off lightly for what was an important 3,000-word essay – and he expressed himself 'delighted' with the Bakst book.

Sitwell's kindness made me feel all the sadder when I read a bad-tempered review of the *Bibliography* in *The Times Literary Supplement*, which made a point of denigrating his essay. He was very angry about it, and sent me a letter apologising for the review which, he said, seemed to be all his fault. But it was not – it was merely the work of a boorish and literal-minded critic; in those days it was frustrating to attempt to understand such an undeservedly bad review, as nothing was signed. Anna summed it up well when she said the *Literary Supplement* 'has no music'.

In addition to the books which I had published before the company was launched, we issued during the next sixteen years a total of fifty-three works, some dealing with subjects never before broached in English, except perhaps for minor magazine references here and there. Other books were in themselves works of art. Some of our most original books were published in very limited editions of around twenty to thirty copies. In these I was able to adapt my skill in miniature painting, for some contained reproductions of line-drawings by myself, which I elaborately coloured and gilded by hand, using watercolour, body colour and shell gold.

One of my concerns in producing such books was to investigate in practice William Blake's method of colouring his relief-etched books, such as *Songs of Innocence* (1789), *America A Prophecy* (1793) and so on. He printed his outlines from relief-etched plates, that is, with the lines of the design left in relief on the plate, and not bitten into it as in ordinary etching. He then coloured them in watercolour in various degrees of elaboration, but in some cases by printing the colour on top of the design from another plate; it was the former that I wished to investigate. I used photo-line blocks for the design, but tried to follow Blake's style of hand-colouring as closely as possible. Inevitably some deviations occurred, but I found it a valuable exercise which demonstrated to me at least that if Blake did all the colouring himself, it would have occupied him, in an octavo copy of average elaboration, some two or three hours a page. In a highly elaborate copy, like the *Songs of Innocence and of Experience* (1794) he made for the barrister and antiquary, Henry Crabb Robinson, this could easily have been tripled or quadrupled. His more simply-coloured copies, realized with washes, could have been done in considerably less than an hour a page.

After working on a couple of books along these lines I turned to less derivative conceptions, one of the first of which was *Gabha* (1964). Its opening words are, 'How can a blacksmith hope, like Blake, to give you the end of a golden string? How can he ask you to wind it into a ball? Yet the hammer and anvil make resounding music beside the fires of night, while the brush and the pen modify'. *Gabha*, which is the Erse word for 'blacksmith', is a kind of modern emblem book described in its prospectus as 'a visionary study in pictures and words.' It was followed by several books similarly conceived and realized.

We also published poetry, among which was a *jeu d'esprit* by Siegfried Sassoon called *An Adjustment* (1955). Its subject was centred on a copy of John Nyren's *Young Cricketer's Tutor* (1833), which he had some years previously presented to Edmund Blunden. Other poetry included *Way* (1969), two poems by Laurence Whistler, illustrated with photographs of an engraved glass goblet entitled *Idea of a City*, which I had commissioned from him as a birthday gift to Pamela; and collections of poems by the undeservedly neglected writer and artist, Mary Stella Edwards, by Thomas Rice Henn, by Edmund Blunden, and a long poem by Francis Warner.

When the idea of publishing the Blunden collection, *Eleven Poems* (1965), was being discussed, Francis Warner brought Edmund to luncheon with us. Though shy, I found him altogether charming; he talked as he thought, and that very faintly so that at times I followed him with difficulty: 'tangential' is the adjective that comes to mind to best describe his conversation. After lunch we retired into my study, and he fell asleep while reading a book of Thomas Flatman's poems that I showed him. He was so still and seemed almost to have ceased breathing that I felt somewhat alarmed in case he was ill, and I touched him on the shoulder, but he awoke at once, full of apologies.

Slightly built and somewhat sharp featured, with bright alert eyes, he resembled a timid little wild creature, an impression accentuated by his extremely untidy clothes. Francis Warner said he was extraordinarily extravagant and had no sense of the value of money. He was eccentric, too, in other ways. Edward Malins (author of the book *Samuel Palmer's Italian Honeymoon*; 1968), took Blunden at about this time to see Blenheim and was highly embarrassed by his insistence on carrying a transistor radio everywhere so that he could listen to the Test Match commentary. Why, I wonder, do so many poets love cricket?

Blunden was one of the pleasantest men I, as a publisher, had to deal with. Generous to a fault, one had to be very firm in refusing his frequent proffered gifts. He had been on a diplomatic mission after World War II to Tokyo, where he lectured widely on English literature and art. When we visited his attractive house by the bridge at Long Melford, Pamela exclaimed in admiration of some beautiful lacquer boxes which he had brought home from Japan. Without hesitation he at once pressed two of them on to her, and when she refused to take them, he assumed she did not like them and tried to give her others instead. She could not possibly accept them, but finally, to pacify him, she accepted a snapshot of Siegfried Sassoon cuddling a cat.

I first met Sassoon in 1954 at the Gosses' Newnham house – they had moved back to Cambridge by this time. In reply to my thanks for being allowed to publish *An Adjustment* he commented, 'Yes, I am sure it will be great fun. And it will in any case be a lesson to the old Jackdaw (Keynes) who tries to monopolise all my publications nowadays. It really is quite a clever little piece – just like Shakespeare'. He lunched at our house soon afterwards (we too had moved again, and were living in a wing of the Court at Meldreth) bringing Anna and Philip with him in a big old-fashioned open motor-car. Philip afterwards told us that he drove at 25 m.p.h. until he came to a built-up area, when he accelerated to 50 m.p.h.

Sassoon differed completely from Blunden. He saw the world in terms of himself, himself as a microcosm of the world. I think essentially he felt unsure of himself, which caused him to over-emphasise his own persona in compensation. After our first meeting, whenever he visited Cambridge, he invited Philip and me to luncheon. At the first of these luncheons, I told him how much I had enjoyed reading his *Memoirs of a Fox-Hunting Man* (1928) despite my dislike of the sport. 'Yes,' he said, 'it really is a very good book; let me tell you how I came to write it...', and he ran on for at least twenty minutes, until he noticed Philip nudging me under the table, at which he turned very red, and we all conversed in embarrassed monosyllables for the remainder of the meal.

Yet Siegfried was very fond of Philip, and I have a letter he wrote to me after Anna died in 1957, begging me to let him know if there was anything he could do for him. Despite his introspection and egocentricity Siegfried had the kindest of hearts and his acts of generosity were legion. Philip was one of the few people who could deflate his egoism, and it says much for Siegfried's good nature that he never really resented it. Philip called Siegfried Sassoon and Sacheverell Sitwell 'our two SSs', and wickedly suggested we should, when the opportunity arose, mix their names on Golden Head title-pages, so that on one the author's name should be given as Sacheverell Sassoon, and on the other as Siegfried Sitwell.

At times Siegfried could be a delightful companion; it became a different matter when he talked of himself or of his work, and half closing his eyes, raised his eyebrows, turned towards the person he was addressing, peering into the distance above his companion's head, preparatory to embarking on a long monologue concerning Sassoon and Sassoonery. Nevertheless, one forgave everything when his rare smile and an expression of intense kindliness lit up his face.

He expressed great doubt whether it would be possible to continue his semi-autobiographical books – *Sherston's Progress* (1936) and so on – because, he said, he had made too many notes, and could no longer see the wood for the trees. And in fact he did not from this time add to them. I mentioned an incident in the *Fox-Hunting Man* that had saddened me: when his groom was killed. But, said Siegfried, he was not really killed at all: he died of tuberculosis after the end of the War. These books seem to be largely interspersed with such poetic licence.

One day, when Siegfried was in Cambridge, I invited him to lunch with me at a local hotel. He replied, yes he could lunch with me, but Philip 'must' be there. So I next day took myself to Newnham to invite Philip to join us. Somewhat embarrassed, he said, 'I have a message for you from Siegfried. He has asked me to tell you that the Royal Hotel is no good, so instead would you, Pamela and Rory (our little son) be his guests at luncheon at the Garden House Hotel'. I just collapsed laughing on to the nearest chair! Such unconscious rudeness could have emanated from nobody but Siegfried. In the circumstances I thought the offer too good to refuse, so asked Philip to accept on our behalf.

We duly lunched with the poet; Anna and Philip, and Philip's daughter Jennifer were also there. Over pre-prandial sherry Siegfried handed Philip a copy of the periodical *Desiderata* which contained an article on the *Fox-Hunting Man*, which he had in places underlined to accentuate the most grandiloquent flattery: 'only to be compared to Tolstoi', 'the Homer of our literature' and so on. Poor Anna, who prided herself on her conversational gifts and gave 'conversation' as her recreation in *Who's Who*, was told peremptorily by Siegfried not to indulge in small talk. In fact he talked only to Philip, Jennifer and myself. When we left the hotel, Philip told Anna about the underlinings in *Desiderata*, and she became so helpless with mirth that we had to assist her all the way through Little St. Mary's Lane.

Yet Siegfried was always worth listening to on the theory of poetry, and on great poets of the past. For instance, he observed that only reality matters in writing; life is a great stream flowing by incessantly and only a few scraps are left on the bank for posterity. All we can ever hope to get is a tiny glimpse of the past, such as Falstaff in Shallow's orchard – a curiosity to us, but everyday life to Shakespeare. These are truths that every writer would do well to heed. And let us make no mistake, Siegfried Sassoon was one of the best English poets of the first half of this century, whatever we think of his *amour propre*.

I have already mentioned briefly Simon Lissim who contributed a concise but graceful essay, 'Bakst as I remember him' to my *Muscovite Peacock*. The Golden Head Press published a richly produced and illustrated monograph on his colourful decorated porcelain. Lissim was an exceptionally resourceful artist and designer who, in addition to his paintings, book illustrations and stage *décors*, designed porcelain for among others La Manufacture National de Sèvres, Claude Boulmé, Lenox China, and Castleton China, as well as silver and jewellery for Carl Sorensen and Son of Copenhagen; in addition he was a gifted and noted teacher. We first met him and his vivacious wife Dorothea in July 1954 when they stayed with us during a tour of Europe.

Simon had been secretary to Georgi Loukomski, the Russian émigré architect, painter and designer. He lived in Paris from 1921 to 1941, during which he knew Diaghilev, Bakst, Benois and many others from the former *Mir Iskusstva* group ('The World of Art', so named from a periodical produced by Diaghilev and his friends in St. Petersburg from 1899 to 1904). Simon gave some piquant thumbnail sketches of these people. Bakst he recalled as genial and kind, always ready to lend a helping hand to anybody. Benois, on the other hand, was completely self-centred and 'would not put two fingers together to help anybody outside the Benois family'; he was, claimed Simon, more historian than artist. As for Diaghilev, Lissim recalled him as a great dandy, who would walk on to the stage between acts, top-hatted, evening-cloaked and monocled, and carrying a gold-topped cane.

Of others on the periphery of the *Mir Iskusstva* group, Simon recalled Anna Pavlova as a highly cultured and educated woman – charming, ladylike and a joy to speak with. Feodor Chaliapin, the great bass, on the other hand conversed like a despot. And when I asked Simon if Ida Rubinstein had been once the mistress of Arthur Guinness he asked in reply 'whose mistress has she not been?'

Simon helped in the preparation of André Levinson's magnificently produced book *Bakst: The Story of the Artist's Life* (1923) and that of *Inedited Works of Bakst* (New York, 1927) by Valerian Svetlov and others. He owned several of the designs reproduced in the Svetlov book, and executed the lettering BAKST on its dust jacket – his first essay in calligraphy.

Lissim's recollections and anecdotes could have filled a book, but two of them are especially worth relating. The first was a recollection of how he was once, during the 1920s, shown by a Parisian dealer a pile of drawings on odd scraps of paper, old envelopes and so on. They were priced at 500 francs apiece (about £5 of our money in those days). But he had not a franc to spare, even though everyone of them was by ...DEGAS!

The second was an incident during the Russian Revolution. Red Army soldiers entered his father's home in Kiev to make a routine search. Having completed this, they demanded something to drink and Lissim *père* took from a cupboard a bottle labelled *Napoléon Cognac* and gave a tot to each soldier. They sipped it several times, and each time spat it on to the carpet, vituperating the Lissims' foul bourgeois taste. 'Funny', said Simon's father, when they had departed, 'That was my best brandy'. 'That's what *you* thought,' said his wife, 'I had filled the bottle with vinegar in case this should happen!'

****

Inevitably I suppose, a few Golden Head dreams failed to come true. Among them were to have been two dance studies: one, an exposition of Laban's kinetography by Albrecht Knust, one of its leading authorities; the other an essay by Rudolf von Laban himself on his theories of dance and movement. Knust actually wrote his book, so I can at least take some credit for having suggested it, but when it was finished it was far too extensive and elaborate for us to produce. It was first published, in English, in two volumes in 1958, by Das Tanzarchiv, Hamburg, under the title *Handbook of Kinetography Laban*. A much more extended, elaborate and well-produced *Dictionary of Kinetography Laban*, also in two volumes, was published in England in 1979 by Macdonald and Evans Ltd., Plymouth, one year after Knust had died. I was saddened to have to decline this great work, but we had neither the capital nor sufficient distributive arrangements to deal with it. Nevertheless, it did lead to an interesting and agreeable acquaintance with Knust himself. A pleasant and unassuming man, small in stature, he seemed to be a diffident version of Sigurd Leeder. He had but one purpose in life: the study, development and dissemination of kinetography, and I still regret that I was unable to help him to realise this.

Soon after discussing Knust's book with him, I went to see Rudolf von Laban himself, in London. Gabor Cossa, the Cambridge antique-dealer and former secretary of the Ballets Jooss, prepared me for the meeting by warning me that, like many another genius, Laban was quite ruthless, and would 'use' anybody for as long as he served a purpose, and would then throw him aside 'like a sucked orange'. Yet Gabor admitted that Laban was probably the most profound thinker the dance had thrown up since Jean-Georges Noverre (1727-1810). My own opinion is that he was even more important than Noverre, who was after all concerned only with ballet, whereas Laban's thought encompassed the whole gamut of human movement. From what I saw of Laban, I should think that Gabor's description was at least somewhat exaggerated – I found him assuredly most charming and friendly. A little above medium build, he had the appearance of a retired army officer or successful man of business. Upright, slim, with a fine head, strong Nordic features and penetrating steely-blue eyes, he looked much younger than his seventy-five years. His hands, though small, looked capable, like those of a sensitive craftsman.

We met at Queen Mary Hall in Great Russell Street, where I found him with his assistant, Lisa Ullmann, nearing the end of one of their large dance-classes. The pupils were predominantly rather plain women, who were, the maestro told me, mostly schoolteachers; of the one or two men, one was a factory hand. The choreography (at least what little I saw of it) looked elegant, and one tended to forget any physical shortcomings in the beauty of the dancers' sinuous waving lines and movements. Laban walked among them making a suggestion here and there, and although his authority appeared obvious, the relationships between master and pupils seemed easy, friendly, co-operative.

After the class I spent a most pleasant couple of hours with Laban, who expressed considerable interest in my past acquaintance with Jenny Gertz, Kurt Jooss and Sigurd Leeder. He spoke with considerable reserve about Jenny, but seemed pleased when I told him I had learned the elements of kinetography, eukinetics and choreutics from Sigurd, and seemed even more delighted that I had commissioned an icosahedron. My idea that Laban should write a short study for the Golden Head Press was tossed into the conversation, and while he seemed quite interested, Miss Ullmann I thought less enthusiastic: when we parted, he promised to think it over and let me know. But unfortunately teaching commitments, and his work on other books previously commissioned, prevented the idea being taken up, and when he died in 1958, nothing further had been done.

A proposal closely related to the dance was to have been a study of the great Russian constructivist stage designer, Alexandra Exter. She had been a close friend of Simon Lissim, who became her artistic executor. In 1930 a set of *pochoirs*, made by Exter herself from her designs, had been issued in Paris by A. Dairov, in a limited edition, accompanied by a hand-written commentary. Only a few were sold, and Simon now had the balance of *pochoirs*, about fifty full sets, which he put at my disposal. But in sending them to me, he made the mistake of putting on the customs declaration an estimate far in excess of their current value, and our Customs levied an import duty on them, so large that if we had paid it and incorporated it into our cover price, we should have been unable to sell a single copy. Now it would be different, for Exter is fully appreciated and much collected; but then it was a different story and, with much regret I had to return them to Simon and abandon the project – one of my greatest regrets from the Golden Head years.

The Golden Head Press ended its activities with the onset of inflation, comparatively mild though it was, in 1970. The costs of printing, and even more of binding, were accelerating far beyond our very limited means, and under these circumstances I did not feel justified in asking my fellow venturers to put up more funds. Our last publication, a charming little jewel of a book, bound in Parisian paper of gold and ultramarine, was *Ardna Gashel* by Olive Cook (1970), illustrated with wood-engravings by her husband Edwin Smith, who was better known as an architect and as one of the most creative photographers of his day. It was a satisfying swan-song.

I was able to return in full the money originally put up by the Golden Head backers. This, after having published fifty-three books of limited marketability, I think not too bad. And although the books were of specialised interest, I hope that within their limitations they served, and in some cases may continue to serve, some useful purpose.

In the late 1970s, a dealer in fine books, Cynthia M. Morris, assembled a complete collection of Golden Head, and pre-Golden Head publications, a considerable achievement, when the extreme limitation of some of the editions is taken into account. This collection was later acquired by Reading University Library, and apart from my own collection, now in the Fitzwilliam Museum Library, it must be unique.

Never able to turn from the love, acquisition or creation of books, I was delighted to be invited to become President of the Private Libraries Association a year after the Golden Head Press ceased publishing. Founded in 1956 for the benefit of owners of private libraries, it has grown steadily in size and influence and has now also become a supporter of small printers and publishers. I have been involved as writer, illustrator or publisher of around a hundred books, so I have done more than the human average to fill collectors' shelves, a thought which pleases me, for a library or even just a selection of good books provides a foundation for civilised living, leading to that wisdom which *The Book of Job* tells us 'is above rubies'.

Since the demise of the Golden Head Press, I have written, designed and produced a few further luxury books, which I have published privately. So far I have published five in some twenty years, and, if my eyesight does not deteriorate, I have high hopes of producing more in the future since they enable me to combine my miniature painting, my writing, my love of books, and above all, my imagination. The first one was *A Title to Phoebe* which was finished in 1972, an essay on the moon in art and life, illustrated with reproductions of four miniatures and one pen-and-ink drawing. Next, in 1974, came *Apollo's Bird* which had no text, but consisted of twelve hand-coloured designs, each giving a different insight into swan mysticism, such as a swan annunciation, trinity, crucifixion, resurrection and final epiphany.

In 1983 I finished what I consider to be the best of my post-Golden Head books: *There Was a Star Danced* ... (1983), an essay on the art of the ballerina, but inspired by and intended primarily as a tribute to Irina Baronova, to whom it was dedicated. It is illustrated with colour reproductions of seven miniatures, one of which, on the title page, depicts Irina with Anton Dolin in *Le Lac des Cygnes*. *There was a Star Danced...* proved to be a happy book in another way, for it initiated for Pamela and me a close and loving friendship with Irina, who is in private life as imaginative, delightful, sparkling and vital as she was in those magical days as a prima ballerina in the Ballet Russe.

Twelve
De Profundis

*

During the first ten years of my venture into publishing, Pamela and I continued to settle down to the full happiness and appreciation of family life, enjoying a relationship reminiscent of Bunyan's Beulah, in which 'the contract between the Bride and Bridegroom was renewed'.

Our son, Rory Brian George, was born in 1952, and our daughter, Delia Fionnuala, in 1958. An extravert from the first, Rory was strongly drawn to all forms of entertainment. Years later he became a student at the Webber-Douglas Academy of Dramatic Art, and after graduating took various jobs from the operation of marionettes for the Da Silva Puppet Company to participation in a circus. While travelling with this circus he achieved something that only he could have done: he lost an elephant. He tethered it outside a pub while he went in for a drink, and returned to find that it had taken itself off. Luckily, after searching for about an hour, he found it in a bus shelter in the company of a terrified courting couple. Rory later became unhappy about the unpredictability of theatrical work, and decided to go into bookselling which has now occupied him for some years.

Delia has also been much occupied with art, after studying at the Byam Shaw Art College. She produces marbled paper, the technique of which she learned from the former head marbler at Sandy Cockerell's bindery; her designs are much more flamboyant than those on the Cockerell papers, being as bright as the wings of a macaw. Appropriately, two of her godparents being the Lissims, some of the chromatic intensity of Simon's designs seem to have inspired her own.

Both Rory and Delia are now happily married, and another generation has begun.

These were all happy future developments, and in the meantime we were able to enjoy the bright imagination of our children. But perhaps we took too much for granted; our mutual love, Pamela's and mine, never faltered, never has faltered, but around it and around our family contentment, a dark spectre began to make its haunting presence felt, and for months I was driven to unmitigated despair. It began with the death of Philip Gosse, who had visited Australia in 1959, after the death of Anna in 1957, and returned much aged, somewhat faded, and lacking much of his characteristic banter.

To mark his homecoming, Geoffrey and Margaret Keynes gave a party in his honour, the pivotal point of which was a spherical cake with the continents marked out in icing, and with a line of icing across the oceans showing the track of Philip's voyage, and on this, in the middle of the Indian Ocean, was placed a model ship heading home from Australia. Geoffrey made a short speech and crowned Philip with a laurel wreath. I have a snapshot taken just after this, showing Philip seated beside Monsignor Alfred Newman Gilbey, which I inscribed 'Philip and the Tempter'. It was Philip's last fling, for soon afterwards, in October, he contracted food poisoning and within a few hours of entering hospital, died.

At the funeral at Cambridge Crematorium I was very upset and had difficulty in preventing my tears from flowing unrestrained. After the service, Geoffrey and Margaret Keynes came over to speak to Pamela and me and (I am sure it was an attempt to cheer me) Geoffrey told us how his brother Maynard had left instructions that his ashes should be placed in King's College Chapel, but that nobody had consulted his will until after they had been scattered elsewhere. Geoffrey laughed heartily at this recollection, but I was in no mood for comfort, for a blackness was beginning to descend on me, a sickness of the soul that was not soon to depart.

Philip's death shocked me quite disproportionately: after all, he was eighty years old and in somewhat frail health, so his demise should not have been altogether unexpected. But it brought on a repetition of the horrid thanatophobia that had smitten me as a schoolboy, but with a strength and an intensity I would not have believed possible. For ten or eleven months it took possession of my soul like an infernal predator, dominating my every thought, even my dreams, with preoccupations of death and decay. I really felt that I was heading for madness and would not be left alone for a minute. I was terrified of sleep, in case I should never awaken. I would walk miles to avoid a cemetery, and if I saw a funeral cortège approaching, I would run away in the opposite direction until my legs would carry me no farther.

Several good friends tried to help me: Arthur Astbury, who had experienced similar horrors; my doctor and old friend, Edward Bevan; the scholar and Unitarian minister, Dr. R.F. Rattray, a man of tremendous intelligence. Above all, and bearing the full brunt of my illness, was Pamela, whom I turned to every hour, and whom I could not bear to be out of my sight; as with everything else in my life, she proved to be my best and wisest friend.

It ended almost as suddenly as it had begun. We were *en route* for Frinton-on-Sea almost a year later, during the following September (we took a house there most summers when the children were young) and I caught a glimpse of a genial wooded landscape in the gentle light of the afternoon sun. For the first time for many months I felt at peace, and knew that the spectre had fled at last.

My neurosis, not surprisingly in view of the form it had taken, turned my mind to the mystery of religion, which had all my life been a vexatious matter, of deep doubt always and with the two poles of Catholicism and Nonconformity dragging me first one way and then another.

In view of the importance of the religious struggle in my life, particularly during my adolescence, it will not be out of place to state, however briefly, at this point, the kind of uncertainty that exercised, still exercises, my mind, and to indicate some of the conclusions, however provisional, I have reached over several decades. First I may say that I find it quite impossible to be certain, at the time I am writing this, where one may look for a satisfactory formal religion, for there are so many contradictions both between them, their teachings and beliefs, and between all of them and the growing resources of scientific knowledge. It is true that some eminent scientists have been and are deeply religious men: Sir Arthur Eddington, Plumian Professor of Astronomy at Cambridge from 1913, and a devout Quaker, and Sir Oliver Lodge, the great physicist and President of the Society for Psychical Research, come to mind at once, and I have known many others, but it is obvious they are a minority. The scepticism of Stephen Hawking is more typical.

A brilliant attempt to wed science and religious belief was made by Pierre Teilhard de Chardin, a Jesuit priest, who expounded his ideas in a series of remarkable books, beginning with *The Phenomenon of Man* (1959). He seems to go much of the way to reconcile Darwinism and evolution with the as yet uncompleted development of the soul of man, making Tennyson's vision seem less of a dream:

> One far-off divine event
> To which the whole creation moves.

I cannot conceive how the cosmos in which we live began unless it was created as an act of will by an unimaginable power, but I can also perceive that there is no reason why eternity should not stretch into the infinite past as well as into the infinite future, making an act of creation unnecessary. Time is possibly a phenomenon apparent only to earthbound beings, with their extremely limited life-span, outside which there is eternity or no-time, without beginning or end, because time is non-existent.

When I consider the ever-growing research in astronomy and cosmography, and the discovery of tremendous objects like the galaxy 3C236, a dot of light in the night sky, which has two outer 'clouds' separated by 20,000,000 light years, with light travelling at 186,283 miles a second, time and space seem no longer relevant. At the other end of the scale is the infinitely small: the atom with a nucleus measuring about two-hundred billionths of a millimetre, so infinitesimal that no man has yet set eyes on it, even with the most powerful microscope. These sizes and distances are terrifying, especially when we are beginning to understand that the cosmos in which we live is possibly but one of many.

Yet despite all such considerations, I remain convinced that there is a mighty spiritual dimension, call it what you will, in the cosmos, and that it affects mankind. Such sublime works of art as Michelangelo's Sistine Chapel frescoes, and his statue of David, Beethoven's *Ninth Symphony* and *Fidelio*, Shakespeare's *King Lear*, Tolstoy's *Anna Karenin*, Blake's *Jerusalem*, and the *Book of Isaiah*, cannot be accounted for simply in psychological, environmental, intellectual or materialistic terms; one must also include the divine spark of inspiration, which must be kindled by a power beyond ourselves.

I do not know if mankind as a whole will ever come to comprehend or understand this, but I am convinced that a few individuals have perceived it, especially some great religious leaders in their pristine innocence before their ideas became exaggerated and their teachings distorted by theologians and others among their followers. I think many artists (I use the word in its widest possible catchment) have probably perceived it also, but by no means all. It is indeed strange that the artist, so often, as I believe, a vehicle for inspiration, should also frequently be unsatisfactory in character. Few stand out like Blake, who remained transparently honest and consistently true to his ideals. In contrast, when I read some of Beethoven's letters to his publishers, his grasping attitude makes me feel quite ashamed. Charles Dickens, undoubtedly an inspired writer and one of the greatest of all novelists, left much to be desired in his treatment of his wife and in other aspects of his private life. It may be that the moral man is not as a rule a satisfactory vehicle for sublime expression in the arts, just as in another sphere, in order to attain sainthood or mystical experience, it is usually necessary for the subject to be weak in spirit and poor in heart. Or it may simply be that highly-developed morality usually leaves little room for the contrasts of artistic expression.

Of a possible hereafter I do not know: logic tells me it is impossible, but logic is of little help in the explanation of spiritual matters. I *hope* that I may live in eternity after the death of my body, but cannot conceive the conditions of such a life. If we shall have no body, sensation as we know it will be impossible; without a brain we could not think, without eyes we could not see, without ears we could not hear, without noses we could not smell, without a tongue we could not taste, and our sense of touch would be impossible without nerves. So whatever it is, if there is such a life, it must be utterly different from that which we experience in the material world. It is unlikely to be a world of heavenly choirs singing praises for all eternity: could anything more boring be imagined? Neither is it likely to emulate Sydney Smith's idea of heaven: eating *pâtés de foie gras* to the sound of trumpets. Perhaps in eternity we shall exist as powers, like the angels visualised by theologians: guardians or guides of pure spirit bringing influence to bear on the living, influence that could be either good or evil, for let us not forget that there are obverse and reverse in all things. But taking everything into consideration, I cannot say that I am convinced that there is individual life outside the body after death; on the other hand I do not altogether dismiss the idea.

Possibilities other than personal survival exist. It may be that the soul returns to a great reservoir of spiritual energy from which all life is kindled. It may even be that such a reservoir is bound up with the very existence of the Deity, which would go a long way towards an explanation of the divine spark, that constant communication with God, which the religious tell us is the essence of humanity. It might be, too, that the whole universe and other universes beyond it, are also parts or aspects of the Godhead, that the expanding universe, about which we are told by scientists, is part of a mighty pulsating being, eternal and enormous beyond conception. The existence of such a vast unimaginable being or Atman could suggest that the creation of man, indeed of the whole natural world as we know it, is the work of a demiurge, such as Blake perceived in the Elohim, a being of pure spirit more insubstantial than the wind, but with a cosmic power of creation, a being who might have developed spontaneously from the all-embracing Atman, yet more finite in time and space. There is much wisdom anent this in the poetry of William Blake, to which I have turned for many years for both understanding and comfort.

Despite all my doubts and difficulties of understanding, I can still say that I firmly believe in the power of prayer. But to whom or to what is one to pray? As the reader will already have gathered, I was raised as a Christian in a Christian ambience, and I therefore pray in a Christian manner to a god of Christian conception. But I see nothing wrong or misguided, if one is brought up in a Buddhist ambience, in praying to a Buddhist god, or a Hindu to any number of the gods in his pantheon. If what I have written about a great all-embracing being, the Atman, the supreme spirit or unknowable supreme universal self, and the possible existence of a creative demiurge, then it must be possible for many demiurges to exist and to receive prayer in different forms and from different concepts.

But for the artist, the act of creation is even more puissant than prayer. To create something, however humble, is a god-like activity, and that is why the maker, the artist, the craftsman is, in terms of the cosmos more important than the mere scholar, thinker or theoretician. As Blake indicated in aphorisms inscribed on his engraving of the *The Laocoön* (*circa* 1820):

A Poet, a Painter, a Musician, an Architect: the Man Or Woman who is not one of these is not a Christian.

You must leave Fathers & Mothers & Houses & Lands if they stand in the way of Art.

Prayer is the Study of Art.
Praise is the Practise of Art.
Fasting &c, all relate to Art.
The outward Ceremony is Antichrist.
The Eternal Body of Man is the Imagination.

In other words true creative work is itself prayer made manifest: every craftsman and artist, be he writer, musician, painter, poet, sculptor, actor, dancer, blacksmith, carpenter, printer, engineer, or what you will, should create with the utmost intensity of his being, for in so doing he reaches out his finger and touches the hand of the eternal spirit.

Thirteen
The Followers of William Blake

*

I have for long been drawn to the circle of young artists who sat at the feet of William Blake during his closing years, treating him as a prophet whose every utterance was inspired and under whose tutelage much of their vision was formed. Calling themselves 'The Ancients' because they were convinced that ancient man was superior in every way to modern man, and with 'Poetry and Sentiment' as their motto, they foregathered regularly to exchange views and criticism. Their leader was Samuel Palmer and the other members of the group included Edward Calvert, George Richmond, Francis Oliver Finch, Welby Sherman, the brothers Frederick and Arthur Tatham, and Henry Walter, each of whom I have written about in large or small studies.

Of these, Calvert was the first whom I studied in depth and, stimulated by Geoffrey Keynes, I wrote my *Edward Calvert* (1962). Geoffrey Keynes advised me to steer clear of whom he called 'the clever but stupid Geoffrey Grigson', who had written a book on Palmer for, he said, he would do everything possible to discourage me, an opinion later proved true, when Grigson tried gratuitously to persuade Oxford University Press not to commission me to edit Palmer's letters. Suffice to say that although *Edward Calvert* did not effect a large sale it brought me a *succès d'estime* in academic circles.

Among academics who took up *Calvert* was the great W.B. Yeats authority, Thomas Rice Henn, a generous and big man in every meaning of the word. Himself a not inconsiderable poet, he fully appreciated and understood the workings of the artistic mind, and felt that I had successfully illustrated this in *Calvert*, as also did his former pupil, the poet and dramatist Francis Warner. An upshot of this was that Henn and Warner, director and deputy director of the W.B. Yeats Summer School at Sligo, invited me to lecture there in 1963 and again in 1964 on the influence of Blake and his young disciples on Yeats's poetry and thought.

Yeats's son, Michael, a senator in the Irish parliament, and his talented wife Gráinne were in Sligo on our second visit. Gráinne's playing of the Irish harp I found hauntingly beautiful, and Pamela and I listened in enchantment when we heard her practising a couple of rooms away from us along our hotel landing, by a window opening on to the balmy sunshine of a western Irish summer. She seemed able to charm the very essence of the Gael from the strings of her instrument.

One evening, local talent assembled to provide a concert in honour of the Summer School. As V.I.P.s we were among those seated in the first row of the stalls among other English visitors, and felt somewhat shaken when a Sligo patriot stepped on to the stage and recited the dying speech of an Irish freedom fighter before being hanged by the brutal British in 1916. Throughout his recitation the performer fixed his eye on the front row of the audience, much to our discomfiture.

A lighter entertainment took the form of a 'Fiddler of Dooney' competition, during which the contestants gave of their best on the stage of a local cinema, against a painted backcloth showing an enormous glass of Guinness's stout, and an assurance in large red capitals that GUINNESS IS GOOD FOR YOU. The fiddlers varied in skill, and performed Irish folk music either nonchalantly or bashfully, with their eyes fixed on the floor in front of them, some accompanying their efforts with great stamps of their feet. This continued for a whole day, but we had as much as we could stand after a couple of hours.

A 'grand parade' wound through the centre of Sligo, headed by the local pipe and drum band dressed in saffron kilts. The bulk of the parade consisted of farm trailers hauled by tractors; on some, accordion bands played popular dance tunes interspersed with traditional Irish melodies; others carried set-pieces and *tableaux vivants* which, though roughly conceived and constructed, showed much ingenuity and imagination. The parade was accompanied by groups of enthusiastic young boys who ran beside the floats cheering and shouting. The traffic stopped neither for the parade nor for the old-age-pensioners' race run through the main street, with all the local dogs in attendance. Yet nobody, competitor or dog, suffered any injury, and motorists, who almost anywhere else in Europe would have been beside themselves with impatience and anger, entered with good-humour into the spirit of the event as the race wove its way among them.

****

After the Calvert book, I wrote several more books and studies of 'The Ancients'. These included the catalogue of the exhibition *Samuel Palmer: a Vision Recaptured,* held at the Victoria and Albert Museum in 1978. The catalogue also included essays by Sir Geoffrey Keynes, Graham Reynolds and Arnold Fawcus, who produced this book and the Blake Trust facsimiles of Blake's illuminated books at his Trianon Press in Paris.

Sometime before this exhibition, Fawcus had asked me if I would compile a catalogue and study of Palmer's etchings and of his designs for the *Eclogues* of Virgil and for the shorter poems of Milton to be published by the William Blake Trust. Geoffrey Keynes, founder of the Trust, gave his blessing to the project, and I readily agreed to the suggestion. I found Arnold difficult and irritating to work with; he was over-enthusiastic and full of conflicting ideas, and neither his own hard work nor mine ever seemed to get us anywhere. He spent many weekends with us, and each time, soon after his arrival, he unpacked his attaché cases and covered my study floor with their contents – endless proofs, trial pages and notes – so that we had to squat among them to work. At the end of the weekend, after exhausting himself, Pamela and me, everything would be repacked and taken back to Paris for further work with the printers. I produced several drafts of my proposed text, none of which satisfied him, and it is certain that they did not satisfy me after his incessant rearrangements. How well I understood the comment of the American collector and Blake Trustee, Lessing J. Rosenwald: 'I would rather work *with* Arnold than *for* him'.

Geoffrey Keynes sometimes came to luncheon with us during these visits, and did not bother to hide his own irritation at Arnold's loquacity, especially when he held us up in the dining room while Geoffrey (who, like most aged people, liked to have his food served promptly) snapped at him to, 'Get on with your lunch, Arnold!' as if he were reproaching a dilatory schoolboy. But there was considerable excuse for poor Arnold, who was already (though I did not suspect it) suffering from the cancer of the bladder shortly to kill him. Probably this debility caused his prevarication. When Arnold died in 1979, he had prepared only the collotype plates for the Samuel Palmer book; my studies were eventually absorbed into my *Catalogue Raisonné of the Works of Samuel Palmer* (1988), so my labours were not wasted. As for the plates, they were issued, unaccompanied by a text, by the William Blake Trust in 1990.

Samuel Palmer is the most interesting of all Blake's followers. I was drawn to him first during the War years because, like so many others, I saw in his youthful work an escapist glimpse into what seemed to be a wonderful past Golden Age, during which war and its horrors would have been little more than a distant shadow. It was as if, like Moses, one was beholding the distant Promised Land from Mount Nebo. I was drawn to him also because his work, or at any rate that part of it which I knew, seemed to extend and underline the miraculous little wood engravings made by Blake for Robert John Thornton's *School Virgil* (1821). These are unique in Blake's *oeuvre* both in technique and insomuch as they were almost his only attempt to depict the English landscape. It was these 'little dells, and nooks, and corners of Paradise' as Palmer called them, which provided him with his point of departure, and which helped to make his own early work a mirror of the inscape of the land. And not only the early work, for despite fashionable prejudices in some circles, Palmer's later paintings and etchings expand and enlarge upon the spirit of his early work.

My first study of Palmer's work took the form of a book on his etchings. A short time after this was published, Francis Warner telephoned me about a cache of Palmer's letters written during his visit to Italy in the late 1830s; they were owned by the Linnell family, descendants of Palmer's father-in-law. Would I, he asked, be prepared to edit them? My reply was affirmative, with the provision that a reasonable agreement could be worked out. In the event I suggested that I should edit all of Palmer's letters, and Francis put me in touch with Oxford University Press, who commissioned the work.

The project kept me busy for the next few years, and finally ran into two volumes and over 1,000 pages (1974). During these years Samuel Palmer became part of my daily life, of my very household and family, a very real presence among us. Though often a delightful and witty companion, at other times he could be irritating beyond measure, wrong-headed, bigoted, weak in the face of his overbearing in-laws, indecisive and self-pitying, yet finally I came to respect him for his devotion to the memory of Blake, and for his supreme artistic integrity.

I wrote two biographies of him. The first was published simultaneously with the letters in 1974, and I now regret that it was written at a time when I was decidedly irritated with him, after I had been working on so many of his letters of middle and later life which spotlighted the less likeable aspects of his nature. I think – and hope – that the second biography published in 1987 restored a more accurate perspective to his life. It was a life during which Palmer created some of the most original works of English landscape art, in which he painstakingly worked on paintings and etchings inspired by the greatest poetry, above all that of Virgil and Milton, and by the influence of the greatest artists, pre-eminently Claude, Titian, Giorgione, Giulio Bonasone, Jakob van Ruisdael and Rembrandt.

In 1975, on the proposal of my friend Jack King, then Bursar of the College, I was appointed a Senior Research Fellow of Wolfson College in the University of Cambridge, so as to facilitate my work on Blake's followers. The most important result of this was my *Catalogue Raisonné of the Works of Samuel Palmer* (1988). For this and my other work on these artists I was awarded a Doctorate of Letters by Cambridge University in 1990.

****

In 1976 I became involved in the official enquiry into the forgeries of Samuel Palmer paintings and drawings made by Tom Keating. I had collected a certain amount of material from auction catalogues and press reports concerning what were claimed to be newly-discovered Palmers: I was sure they were not his work but was puzzled by them, for they had obviously been made by somebody who was at least familiar with Palmer's compositions. I was just beginning to gather material for my *Catalogue Raisonné*, and was planning to list them in an appendix of forged and doubtful works. At about the same time, my friend David Gould, a noted expert, wrote to ask me if I had seen the so-called Palmers. He emphasised that they were rubbish, and asked if I would help *The Times* salesroom correspondent, Geraldine Norman, who wanted to write an article about them. I agreed at least to give her access to my records, and she pressed on with her enquiries, which finally led her to Keating and to his exposure.

How these daubs ever came to be accepted as genuine I cannot begin to understand. They came on to the London art market, not exactly in droves, but in considerable numbers, which fact alone should have alerted everybody, for the sudden appearance of a master's work in such quantity is always suspicious. Despite this they were accepted as genuine by certain dealers, auction houses and art historians, who seem to have been blinded by the plausible provenance attributed to them, also the work of the resourceful Keating. I have previously been taken to task for mentioning in print the names of some of those, living or dead, who were allegedly or actually misled, so without apologising for that, I will refrain from doing so again, for I am, I hope, no Don Basilio, bent on initiating a whispering zephyr of scandal. Those who wish to know more may consult *The Fake's Progress* (1977) by Keating and others.

The Keatings were in fact crudely slapped-on caricatures of Palmer's sensitive and animated drawing and brushwork, and should not have befooled anybody with a minimum of connoisseurship. But that is exactly what these experts did not have; the forgeries were judged by their apparent provenance and by the dirty labels with which Keating had thoughtfully adorned them, and by the dust which he had introduced underneath the glass of the frames. Art history is splendid, but unaccompanied by sensitive connoisseurship it can mislead, as was amply demonstrated in this case – especially when the condition of works painted in oil was taken into consideration: their surfaces were still tacky. This ought to have raised a question in the mind of anybody familiar with paintings, for if they had really been painted during the Shoreham years, nearly a century and a half before they were 'discovered', they would have been as hard as rock. Yet some of these forgeries changed hands for thousands of pounds apiece. I must, however, record that in most, if not in all cases, dealers and auctioneers, as soon as they realised the true position, honourably refunded in full what they had been paid.

I am not sure that the Crown was wise to prosecute Keating, for the notoriety surrounding the trial gave him and his work undue importance. Anyway, the trial ended when his health showed signs of deterioration, which may have suggested to some that the prosecution was unsure of its case and therefore seized on an excuse to drop it, although I am sure that this was not so, for excellent available evidence would, I feel certain, have won a verdict for the prosecution.

I appeared as an expert witness for the prosecution, and demonstrated that Keating's work, even if it had been skilfully painted, consisted at best of a series of pastiches. In one composition, for instance, a view of Sepham Barn (Palmer's original *The Valley of Vision: Sepham Barn, Shoreham*, 1828, is in the Yale Center for British Art), he mistook Palmer's rendering of a nearby haystack as an extension of the barn itself, and added a door to its side. In another, which he called *Shoreham at Twilight*, he borrowed almost the entire composition from Palmer's *Pastoral with a Horse-Chestnut*, painted about 1831-32, in the Ashmolean Museum, Oxford. Keating's *Barn at Shoreham* was similarly filched from Palmer's *Cart Shed and Lane* of 1828, in the Victoria and Albert Museum. Altogether a sorry story.

During ensuing years Keating's work has been on the market, seen by some as good investment material. It is advertised in the kind of terms that ought to be reserved for the work of masters, not for that of a poor copyist of other painters' styles. Those unwise enough to buy these paintings will surely regret it, for when its notoriety has worn off the work will be seen for what it is: worthless rubbish, at best evidence of human gullibility.

Fourteen
Dolce Vita

In 1967 we moved once more, this time to a country house in seven acres of grounds where we stayed for a quarter of a century. It had begun life in 1836 as a miller's cottage, but over the intervening years had been extended to become a fairly commodious country house. In the grounds we found a cottage, the remains of a large windmill of brick construction which called to mind a Martello tower, and several other less attractive buildings, most of which we pulled down. But interesting possibilities were suggested to me by one remaining structure, a small cowshed, and this I left intact. In time we transformed it into a tiny theatre, seating an audience of thirty-five, after lots of work, effort and expense, even though it was far from luxurious, even spartan in its finish and decoration. But I thought it well worth all the trouble.

We arranged one, sometimes two, theatre evenings each summer and they came to conform to a pattern: the performance usually comprised two parts, with an hour between for refreshments and conversation. Performances began at 8 p.m. and usually finished by 10.30 p.m. Music predominated, but there were also poetry readings, films, drama and other forms of entertainment.

In the summer of 1987, we celebrated our Ruby Wedding anniversary, and part of the entertainment was a harpsichord recital in the theatre by the virtuoso performer, Gerald Gifford. He composed, especially for the occasion, two short pieces dedicated to Pamela and me, entitled *Pamela's Pleasure* and *Raymond's Relish*: the former a delicate piece, the latter a more bombastic composition – a couple of latterday *Enigma Variations*.

It was our thirty-second theatre entertainment since performances began in October 1969. Earlier presentations had included, among other things, a reading by John Beech of poetry published by the Golden Head Press, chamber music (including several recitals on various instruments by Gerald Gifford), programmes by Clive Webster based on the life and work of Dylan Thomas, a recital by Alan Chedzoy of poetry by William Barnes of Dorset, and a most original Victorian magic-lantern entertainment by the highly versatile Edwin Smith and Olive Cook.

David Parsons, looking as if he had stepped out of a miniature by Hilliard, gave a recital of lute music, supplemented by a few pieces on the early 19th-century dital harp which usually stands silent in our drawing room. It is a pretty instrument invented by Edward Light (1747-1832), redolent of a Regency interior, part lute, part guitar and part harp, decorated in black and gold surmounted with the figure of a benevolent eagle. We also put on several Victorian toy theatre performances, one given by Alan Powers, assisted by Peter Davidson and others, when in 1981 they presented the Victorian spectacle *The Battle of Waterloo* (1824), based on 'Mr. Astley's production'. Two performances were given by the doyen of 'Penny Plain, Twopence Coloured', George Speaight, the first being *The Sleeping Beauty in the Wood* (1849), and the second *The Corsican Brothers; or, The Fatal Duel* (1852). In each George used characters and scenery cut out of the original 19th-century published paper sheets.

I never cease to be astonished at how convincing these performances were. George does everything himself – voices, movements, 'business' (including elaborate 'transformations'), and the operation of a Victorian musical box which provides themes for ballet, and 'atmosphere' during intervals and pauses. George is more than a performer, he is a genius: apart from any other consideration this is demonstrated by the fact that, though he does everything in full view of the audience, one's eyes remain glued to the tiny stage, oblivious of his presence. To watch a performance by George is to witness a *tour-de-force* of performing art, its effect startling in the curious medium he has chosen. You can really believe that you are inside one of the old Victorian playhouses – Astley's, Covent Garden, Surrey, Drury Lane, Coburg, Lyceum – witnessing a live performance.

****

Now that I have attained more than the biblical threescore and ten years, I feel that I am justified in looking back over my life in order to make some kind of assessment. I have enjoyed most of it, but here and there less than enjoyable periods occurred – during visitations of neurosis, during puberty, and for much of my schooldays, but these things apart, I have been happy, and especially so during the forty-odd years of our marriage.

There are few things I would change, given the opportunity, but I have some reservations about my business life. I much enjoyed being a director of the family firm when we practised the traditional crafts of architectural metalworking, but when for reasons I have already explained, this was dropped and everything in the family firm became focussed on mechanical engineering, my interest diminished. I am not wishing to say that such work does not demand craftsmanship, but it is not an aspect of craftsmanship which attracts me. I incline rather to the view of Blake: 'A Machine is not a Man nor a Work of Art; it is destructive of Humanity & of Art.'

The blacksmith, the whitesmith, the brassworker, the bronzesmith, the repoussé worker – these and other related trades had an almost pastoral origin reaching back to Tubalcain, the first artificer in metal, in *Genesis*. Early metalworkers provided the tiller of the soil with his plough, the shepherd with his staff and the forester with his adze. In historical times, but using the same tools and equipment used by his biblical predecessors, the metalworker has made grilles, weather vanes and finials for great buildings, magnificent gates and screens of wreathed and beaten iron, to terminate prospects and to provide vistas; or brass memorial plates to commemorate the underlying dead; or steel sword blades, damascened with filigree designs in gold for princes to carry in ceremonial parades. How can any work of a mechanical craft, however ingeniously designed, however accurately made, compare with works of this kind? It is not merely a difference of form of

155

approach but a difference of kind, the essential difference between a projection of the mind and a projection of the soul.

As to the perfect life, it is certain that perfect living becomes less and less of a possibility as mankind moves from century to century, from age to age. Yet one does sometimes meet people who have come near to it on their own terms. The gifted etcher, Robin Tanner, who died in 1988, and his wife Heather attained a measure of it in their life in their almost numinous Arts-and-Crafts house in Wiltshire, built on land associated with the 19th-century parson and diarist, Francis Kilvert. Robin was one of H.M. Inspectors of Schools, but having retired from that, he spent every available hour designing, biting and printing new etchings, and illustrating books with his drawings, some of them written by Heather. Together this happy couple printed Robin's etchings on their own press, pulling with loving care impressions of the highest quality. By candlelight in an otherwise darkened room, Robin minutely inspected each impression to ensure its flawlessness, and to see it coruscating with what Samuel Palmer called 'those thousand little luminous eyes which peer through a linear etching, and in those of Claude are moving sunshine upon dew, or dew upon violets in the shade'. What could be more satisfying than to spend one's life in such creation?

Some years ago there lived at Caversham in Suffolk an elderly couple, whose home was a converted mill situated far from any other abode. The man was Alfred Blundell, a former railway porter who, when thus employed, hung watercolours he had painted in the station waiting-room. One day a prominent Royal Academician, who had arrived at the station with time to spare, caught sight of Blundell's watercolours, and was immediately aware that they were the work of a natural talent. He enquired after the artist, Blundell presented himself, and the upshot was that the Academician saw to it that he was able to attend the Slade School for proper instruction. In course of time, Blundell became a noted etcher, and although his work never equalled that of Tanner, it is none the less very good. So, too, is his engraved glass, a medium he was inspired to take up by the example of Laurence Whistler.

Along with art, contentment with the rustic mode entered the inner being of Blundell and his wife, who wove tweed and made his clothes; in Blundell's case, knickerbocker suits (recalling a past age, but eminently practical) which imparted a grave dignity to him. They had no bathroom and when, during the summer, they wanted to bathe, Alfred dug a hole in the garden, lined it with heather, and filled it with clear water from a nearby stream. What happened in winter I know not: perhaps Mrs Blundell would have said, as Kate Blake said of William, his 'skin don't dirt'. But under a soft summer sun, what could be more appealing than an open-air heather-lined bath?

I think, too, of John Wemmick in *Great Expectations*, with his tiny and highly ornamental Gothic cottage, approached over a drawbridge which, once he was home, was raised to keep out the hurly-burly of the world. And I think as often of Jim Ede's lovely art-filled retreat, Kettle's Yard in Cambridge, an example of how a setting for a man of contemplative mind may still be attained in the modern world, even within an urban ambience.

I find much attraction in such attitudes to life, and there are times when I long for Samuel Palmer's 'primitive cottage feeling'. But my own ideal of the desirable life, one I am glad to say I not altogether failed to attain, is a rural Petrarchian existence, of artistic creation and appreciation, in a not over-large country villa, islanded within enough land to provide a belt of quietude, in which one might read, think, write or paint without urban noises and interruptions. It is becoming ever more difficult to find such conditions, though we found them in our own rural homestead which, when we first moved into it, was a paradise of quiet, of sweet breezes, dappled sunshine and gentle showers. Here we grew our old-fashioned roses – William Lobb, Rosa Mundi, Tour de Malakoff, Belle de Crécy, Hebe's Lip, Belle Isis – to say nothing of such delights as parrot tulips, carnations, Irish primroses, lilies, herbs of all sorts, fritillaries, and arbutus. We could sit together in one of the secret seats, reading poetry and breathing the thyme-laden air, or lie at full length in the orchard listening to the bees, surrounded by wild orchids, and watch long-tailed tits making their swooping, darting flights among the apple blossom.

Now, over twenty-five years later, although these delights are still there even if much diminished, the pleasure of savouring

157

them becomes vitiated with increasing acceleration by the noise of aircraft and of road traffic, farm machinery and of motor-cycles racing about, often illegally in nearby bridleways. Insects have multiplied extraordinarily, horrid little black flies which get into your hair, ears and eyes, and even penetrate behind the glass of the frames of prints and watercolours and between the pages of books. Even the weather worsens; we are constantly reminded of this by the media, but little more than a glance is needed to show us the dry ditches, streams, even rivers, trees dying for want of water, the wildlife poisoned by rubbish sprayed on to the land to 'improve' crops, hedges grubbed up (for long with ministerial encouragement) and robbing birds of nesting places and small mammals of shelter.

One could continue this lamentation endlessly. In our case it came to this, that we made our escape and returned to the city, for at least in the case of our city, Cambridge, with its groves of academe, its arcadian meadows and streams, life is quieter, less disturbing and less depressing than in its surrounding countryside. This is not altogether true, I know, of every district in Cambridge, which outside its ancient centre and contiguous areas, contains, like every other town in this island, some depressing modern developments. But there can be no argument that its finest areas are both genial and superb. So when an unusually attractive architect-designed house in what may be called the university area was on offer, we decided to acquire it and leave our rural and rather declined paradise. Here we try to make a scholarly and artistic urban sanctuary with our books and works of art surrounding us. Our former somewhat extensive grounds have been exchanged for a small but attractive and well-established garden, which contains a few beautiful and mature trees, as well as (blessed token!) a grape vine growing on a sunny fence. We no longer have a theatre, but we have our memories, supported by such theatre ephemera as posters, programmes, photographs, designs for costumes and décors – in addition to books on those arts which, brought together, form the composite art of ballet.

We can still indulge in many of our tried and loved pleasures. For Pamela and me, one of our most precious relaxations is to sit together in the evening after a day of satisfying work, Pamela embroidering while I read aloud to her, mostly from Dickens, sometimes from the Sitwells, sometimes from Tennyson, Keats or Blake. Other evenings, particularly during winter, will probably find us poring over books or prints, savouring a favourite volume with an attractive binding, or with an interesting inscription, or annotation, or merely a signature of its author, or its illustrator, or perhaps that of an interesting former owner. There is enchantment in handling a copy of *Alice's Adventures in Wonderland* or *Through the Looking Glass* with an inscription by Dodgson on the flyleaf to one of his little-girl friends; or a copy of *The Wind in the Willows* inscribed by Kenneth Grahame to his sister Helen, who was probably his model for Selina in *The Golden Age*; or books of poems by Spenser or Cowley, once owned by Samuel Palmer at Shoreham, and bearing his signature and annotations; or a letter in the hand of the Duke of Wellington; or a cookery book given by the Ladies of Llangollen to their maid, Mary Carryll, and so inscribed.

As for prints, what a world of imagination may be set in train by handling an impression of an etching by Samuel Palmer with his signature and notes in the margin; of similarly annotated and signed proofs by Robin Tanner, F.L. Griggs or Joseph Webb; of a rare, perhaps unique wood engraving by Thomas Sturge Moore. Every time a work of art is examined and studied, one is struck by something previously unrealised. For good books and works of art are of infinite depth, of endless suggestion, of inexpressible sublimity. One could spend the whole of one's life studying one great work of art, such as Giorgione's *Tempesta* in the Gallerie dell'Accademia, Tintoretto's *Crucifixion* in the Scuola Grande di San Rocco, Veronese's decorations in the 16th-century church of S. Sebastiano, all in Venice, loveliest of cities. Such complete absorption cannot perhaps be claimed for a Palmer etching or a wood-engraving by Calvert, yet there is much more in them than at first meets the eye, and I can only say that such works never tire me, and every time I examine them, they present some new hitherto unsuspected feature – perhaps no more than a line or a shadow – to enrich my experience.

Would I have been able to appreciate and validate such

nuances if my past life had been different? I cannot say, but I can look back over fully three quarters of a century, and can say that my life has been full and that I have enjoyed it, my experience has been wide and I have much to be thankful for. Above all I love and am loved. What more, after all, could I ask?

BIOGRAPHICAL NOTES

1919 –   Born 28th March, Cambridge

1927 –   St. John's College Choir School (until 1929)

1929 –   Cambridge and County High School for Boys (until 1934)

1934 –   Apprenticeship with George Lister and Sons Ltd (until 1939)

1940 –   Director of George Lister and Sons Ltd

1940 –   Forms and directs amateur dance group (until 1944)

1946 –   Associate of the Royal Society of Miniature Painters, Sculptors and Gravers

1947 –   Marries Pamela Helen Brutnell

1948 –   Member of the Royal Society of Miniature Painters, Sculptors and Gravers

1952 –   Birth of son, Rory Brian George

1952 –   Director of Brian Lister (Light Engineering) Ltd, makers of sports/racing motor cars (until 1990)

1953 –   Forms the Golden Head Press Ltd.

1955 –   Member of the Society of Miniaturists

1957 –   Liveryman of the Worshipful Company of Blacksmiths and Freeman of the City of London

1958 –   Birth of daughter, Delia Fionnuala

1962 –	One-man exhibition of paintings *Penetralia Mentis*,
	Galleries of the Federation of British Artists,
	London

1963 –	One-man exhibition of paintings *Homage to Fionnuala*,
	Galleries of the Federation of British Artists,
	London

1965 –	One-man exhibition of paintings *Moonlight and Shades*,
	Galleries of the Federation of British Artists,
	London

1970 –	President of the Royal Society of Miniature Painters,
	Sculptors and Gravers (until 1980)

1971 –	President of the Private Libraries Association (until
	1974)

1971 –	Honorary Senior Member, University College (now
	Wolfson College), Cambridge (until 1975)

1972 –	Governor of the Federation of British Artists (until
	1980)

1975 –	M.A. (Cantab.)

1975 –	Senior Research Fellow, Wolfson College, Cambridge
	(until 1986)

1975 –	President, Architectural Metalwork Association (until
	1977)

1976 –	Chairman of Board of Governors, Federation of British
	Artists (until 1980)

1978 –	Director of John P. Gray and Son Ltd., craft
	bookbinders, Cambridge (until 1982)

1980 – Member of Court of Assistants, Worshipful Company of Blacksmiths, London (until present day)

1981 – A Syndic of the Fitzwilliam Museum, Cambridge (until 1989)

1986 – Emeritus Fellow, Wolfson College, Cambridge (until present day)

1989-90 – Prime Warden, Worshipful Company of Blacksmiths, London

1990 – Litt. D. (Cantab.)

BOOKS AND PAMPHLETS by RAYMOND LISTER

Theodosius on Colour and the Dance Société des Ballets Ivanov, Cambridge 1942

* *The British Miniature* Sir Isaac Pitman and Sons Ltd, London 1951

* *A Bibliographical Check-list of Works by Philip Gosse* John P. Gray and Son Ltd., Cambridge 1952

A Title-List of Books on Miniature Painting Privately published, Linton 1952

* *Silhouettes* Sir Isaac Pitman and Sons Ltd, London 1953

Books at Bedtime Golden Head Press, Cambridge 1953

Thomas Gosse: A Biographical Sketch of an Itinerant Miniature Painter of the Early Nineteenth Century, Golden Head Press, Linton 1953

* *The Muscovite Peacock: A Study of the Art of Léon Bakst* Golden Head Press, Meldreth 1953

Decorated Porcelains of Simon Lissim Golden Head Press Ltd, Cambridge 1955

* *Saint George* Privately published, Cambridge 1955

* *Decorative Wrought Ironwork in Great Britain* G. Bell and Sons Ltd, London 1957

The Loyal Blacksmith Golden Head Press Ltd, Cambridge 1957

Tiddlers, or the Arte of Fishing for Sticklebacks Sette of Odd Volumes, London 1958

* Virgil's *Second Eclogue* Golden Head Press Ltd, Cambridge 1958

* *Alphabet of Movements of the Human Body* by V.I. Stepanov (translated from the French by R.L.) Golden Head Press Ltd, Cambridge 1958

* *Decorative Cast Ironwork in Great Britain* G. Bell and Sons Ltd, London 1960

* *The Song of Fionnuala and Nine other Songs* by Thomas Moore Golden Head Press Ltd, Cambridge 1960

* *The Craftsman Engineer* G. Bell and Sons Ltd, London 1960

Private Telegraph Companies of Great Britain and their Stamps Golden Head Press Ltd, Cambridge 1961
(*Awarded bronze medal diploma at the British Philatelic Exhibition, London 1965, and Diploma de Medalla de Plata at Exposición Filatélica Internacional, Buenos Aires 1962*)

* *Ehon: a Nocturne in Wood and Words* Golden Head Press Ltd, Cambridge 1962

* *Scroll of Proverbs* Golden Head Press Ltd, Cambridge 1962

Edward Calvert G. Bell and Sons Ltd, London 1962

Simon Lissim Interviewed Golden Head Press Ltd, Cambridge 1962

* *The First Book of Theodosius* Golden Head Press Ltd, Cambridge 1962

* *Perennia* by Francis Warner Golden Head Press Ltd, Cambridge 1962

* *Great Craftsmen* G. Bell and Sons Ltd, London 1962

The Miniature Defined Golden Head Press Ltd, Cambridge 1963

* *The Song of Theodosius* Golden Head Press Ltd, Cambridge 1963

* *Gabha* Golden Head Press Ltd, Cambridge 1964

* *Ghazal* Golden Head Press Ltd, Cambridge 1964

* *Tao* Golden Head Press Ltd, Cambridge 1965

Beulah to Byzantium The Dolmen Press, Dublin 1965

How to Identify Old Maps and Globes G. Bell & Sons Ltd, London 1965

The Illuminator. A Tribute to Albert Cousins Golden Head Press Ltd, Cambridge 1966

Victorian Narrative Paintings Museum Press Ltd, London 1966

College Stamps of Oxford and Cambridge Golden Head Press Ltd, Cambridge 1966
(*Awarded silver medal diploma at British Philatelic Exhibition, London 1967, and bronze medal at the International Philatelic Exhibition, London 1970*)

* *The Craftsman in Metal* G. Bell and Sons Ltd, London 1966

* *Inrey* Golden Head Press Ltd, Cambridge 1967

Great Works of Craftsmanship G. Bell and Sons Ltd, London 1967

William Blake: An Introduction to the Man and to his Work G. Bell and Sons Ltd, London and New York 1968

Samuel Palmer and his Etchings Faber and Faber Ltd, London 1969

* *The Emblems of Theodosius or the Unity of Endymion and Prometheus* Golden Head Press Ltd, Cambridge 1969

Hammer and Hand. An Essay on the Ironwork of Cambridge Cambridge University Press, Cambridge 1969

Antique Maps and their Cartographers G. Bell and Sons Ltd, London 1970

* *A Title to Phoebe* Privately published, Cambridge 1972

British Romantic Art G. Bell and Sons Ltd, London 1973

* *Apollo's Bird* Privately published, Cambridge 1974

The Letters of Samuel Palmer (2 vols. Edited by R.L.) Clarendon Press, Oxford 1974

Samuel Palmer, a Biography Faber and Faber Ltd, London 1974

Infernal Methods: A Study of William Blake's Art Techniques G. Bell and Sons Ltd, London 1975

* *For Love of Leda* Privately published, Cambridge 1976

Great Images of British Printmaking Robin Garton, London 1978

Samuel Palmer: A Vision Recaptured by Arnold Fawcus, Sir Geoffrey Keynes, R.L., and Graham Reynolds William Blake Trust, London 1978

Illuminated Manuscripts by Albert Cousins Fitzwilliam Museum, Cambridge 1979

Samuel Palmer in Palmer Country (with topographical notes by A.K. Astbury) Hugh Tempest Radford, East Bergholt 1980

Dance Notation: A Historical View Fitzwilliam Museum, Cambridge 1980

George Richmond: A Critical Biography Robin Garton Ltd, London 1981

* *Bergomask* Privately published, Cambridge 1982

* *There Was a Star Danced...* Privately published, Cambridge 1983

Samuel Palmer and 'The Ancients' Cambridge University Press, Cambridge 1984

Prints and Printmaking: A Dictionary and Handbook of the Art in Nineteenth Century Britain Methuen London Ltd, London 1984

The Paintings of Samuel Palmer Cambridge University Press, Cambridge 1985

The Paintings of William Blake Cambridge University Press, Cambridge 1986

Samuel Palmer: His Life and Art Cambridge University Press, Cambridge 1987

Catalogue Raisonné of the Works of Samuel Palmer Cambridge University Press, Cambridge 1988

British Romantic Paintings Cambridge University Press, Cambridge 1989

Stenochoreography or the Art of Writing Dancing Quickly by Arthur Saint-Léon (translated from the French by R.L.) Privately published, Cambridge 1992

Titles marked with an asterisk contain illustrations by R.L.

Magazine articles, book reviews, introductions and contributions to encyclopedias are not included in the foregoing list.

Relevant publications

The Art of Raymond Lister by Simon Lissim. With a foreword by
L.G.G. Ramsey, Editor of *The Connoisseur* John P. Gray
and Son Ltd, Cambridge 1958

Raymond Lister. Five Essays by Charles Richard Cammell, Peter
Foster, Simon Lissim, L.G.G. Ramsey, Francis Warner
Golden Head Press, Cambridge 1963

INDEX

ABSALOM, 6

A.D.C. THEATRE, Cambridge, 96, 99, 108

ADJUSTMENT, AN by Siegfried Sassoon, 128, 130

ADMIRALTY, 1, 85, 98

ADONIS, 126

ADVENTURES OF THE BLACK GIRL IN HER SEARCH FOR GOD by George Bernard Shaw, 63

ALADDIN, pantomime, 115

ALBANY, Piccadilly, London, 124

ALDWYCH FARCES, 79

ALEXANDER, Russell George, 107

ALEXANDRIA, 59

ALICE'S ADVENTURES IN WONDERLAND by Lewis Carroll (C.L. Dodgson), 44, 119, 124, 159

ALMA-TADEMA, *Sir* Lawrence, 106

AMERICA A PROPHECY by William Blake, 128

'ANCIENTS, THE', 145-152

ANGLESEY ABBEY, Cambridgeshire, 104

ANIMALS (see also DOGS), 16, 22, 23, 109, 115-116, 158

ANNA KARENIN Novel by Lev Tolstoy, 142

ANWAR, Rafiq, 99

APOLLO'S BIRD, by Raymond Lister, 137

ARCHITECTURAL METALWORK, 66-67, 102-105, 155

ARCHIVES INTERNATIONALES DE LA DANSE, Paris, 124

ARDNA GASHEL by Olive Cook and Edwin Smith, 136

ARISTOPHANES, 80, 124

ARNOLD, Annie Elizabeth (my grandmother), 14-15, 43, 76

ARNOLD, Cecilia (my great-grandmother), 11

ARNOLD, Charles (my great-grandfather), 11

ARNOLD, Charles, *junior*, 12, 18

ARNOLD, Constance, 16, 19, 36, 77

ARNOLD, Dod, 17-18

ARNOLD, Dora, 17

ARNOLD, Ellen (my step-great-grandmother), 11

ARNOLD, Elsie, 17

ARNOLD, George, 35

ARNOLD, Hilda, 18

ARNOLD, Jack, 16, 17, 19, 23, 35

ARNOLD, John (my grandfather), 11, 12-19 *passim*, 57, 76

ARNOLD, Mary Ann, 15-16

ARNOLD, Max, 13, 17, 21

ARNOLD, Patrick, 12

ARNOLD, Ruby, 17, 19, 34, 36, 74

ARNOLD, Thomas David (my grandfather's brother), 12, 13, 15-16, 17

ARNOLD, Tom (brother of Max), 21

ARNOLD, Tom (my uncle), 72

ARNOLD, William, 17

ART OF DANCING by Kellom Tomlinson, 89

ARTS THEATRE, Cambridge, 16, 80, 85, 90, 93

ARTS THEATRE RESTAURANT, Cambridge, 87, 93

ASHMOLEAN MUSEUM, Oxford, 151

ASHTON, *Sir* Frederick, 91

ASTBURY, Arthur K., 95, 119, 126, 140

ASTLEY, Philip, 154

ASTLEY'S ROYAL AMPHITHEATRE, London, 155

ASTRONOMY, 61, 141, 143

ATMAN, 143, 144

'AUCASSIN AND NICOLETTE', 82

AUSTEN, Jane, 86, 109, 120

AUSTRALIA, 11, 41-42, 79, 139

AYLING, Joan, 106

BACON BROTHERS, Tobacconists, Cambridge, 30

BAKEWELL, Robert, 103

BAKST, Léon, 124, 127, 132

BAKST. THE STORY OF THE ARTIST'S LIFE by André Levinson, 133

BALANCHINE, Georges, 84

BALDWIN, *Canon* Edward Curtis, 40

BALLET, 80, 81, 83-99 *passim*, 101, 109, 158

BALLET RAMBERT, 85

BALLET RUSSE DE MONTE CARLO, 83

BALLET RUSSE DU COLONEL W. DE BASIL, 83, 137

BALLETS JOOSS, 85-87, 134

BALL IN OLD VIENNA, Ballet by Kurt Jooss, music by Joseph Lanner, 86

BALLYNAHINCH, Co. Tipperary, 11

BAND, H.C.C. ('Dickie'), 79, 120, 121

BARHAM, R.H., 40

BARN AT SHOREHAM, pastiche by
Tom Keating, 151
BARNES, William, 154
BARONOVA, Irina, 84, 137
BASS, Mrs., 43
BAUHAUS, Weimar, 90
BAX, Clifford, 116, 124-126
B.B.C., 99
'BEATTY, Admiral' (steam engine), 28
BEAUCHAMPS, Charles-Louis, 89
BEDELLS, Jean, 93
BEECH, John, 154
BEERBOHM, Sir Max, 116-117
BEETHOVEN, Ludwig van, 20, 142
BEETON, Mrs. Isabella, 9, 20
'BEGGARSTAFF BROTHERS', (pseu-
donym of Sir William Nicholson
and James Pryde when working
together), 23
BEHAM, Bartel, 100
BELGRADE THEATRE, Coventry, 103
BELL, Peter M., 94
BENDIGO, Victoria, Australia, 11, 12
BENESH, Rudolph, 88-89, 90
BEN HUR by Lew Wallace, 41
BENNETT, Vivienne, 78
BENOIS, Alexandre, 124, 132
BERK, Ernst and Lotte, 98-99
BETJEMAN, John, 75
BEULAH, 138
BEVAN, Dr. Edward V., 140
BEWICK, Thomas, 40
BIBLE, 5, 6, 8, 60
BIBLE PICTURES FOR LITTLE
PEOPLE by 'Uncle Harry', 6
BIBLIOGRAPHY OF THE FIRST EDI-
TIONS OF PHILIP HENRY GOSSE
F.R.S. by Peter Stageman, 127
BIEDERMEIER STYLE, 86
BIG BEN, 22
'BIRDCAGE, THE', 103
BIZET, Georges, 54
BIZZARIE DI VARIE FIGURE ... by
Giovanni Battista Bracelli, 90, 95
BLACKMORE, R.D., 94
BLACKSMITHERY, 64-67 passim, 102-
105 passim, 128, 155-156
BLAKE, Catherine (Kate), 157
BLAKE, William, 44, 46, 49, 73, 81,
100, 120, 128, 142, 143, 144, 145-146,
148, 155, 157, 159
BLENHEIM, 129
BLOOMSBURY CIRCLE, 92
BLUNDELL, Alfred, 156-157
BLUNDEN, Edmund, 128, 129, 130

BODLEIAN LIBRARY, Oxford, 79
BOLES, John, 49
BONASONE, Giulio, 100, 149
BOOK OF EVERLASTING THINGS
Edited by Arthur Mee, 46
BOOK OF ISAIAH, 142
BOOK OF JOB, 136
BOOKS, 9, 22, 60-61, 99, 109, 123-137
passim, 145-146
BOOKS AT BEDTIME by Raymond
Lister, with an essay by Philip
Gosse, 119
BORTH, near Aberystwyth, 55
BOSQUET, LE, Ballet by Hans Züllig,
music by Rameau, 86
BOULMÉ, Claude, 132
BOURNEMOUTH, 71
BOYLE, Robert, 120
BOY SCOUT TROOP, 7th Cambridge,
54-5
BRACELLI, Giovanni Battista, 90, 95
BRANCH, Harry, 64
BRIDGE, THE by Nea Walker, 26
BRIGHTON, 71, 90
BRINKLEY, Cambridgeshire, 120
BRITISH MINIATURE, THE by Ray-
mond Lister, 124
BRITTEN, Benjamin, 79
BROOKE, Rupert, 14, 119
BROWN, Alfie, 38
BROWN, Emily, 23
BROWN, Harry ('Noddy'), 53
BRUTNELL, Pamela. See Pamela Lister
BUBBLES, Weekly for Children, 37
BUCKFAST ABBEY, 73
BUNYAN, John, 41, 138
BURGER, Selma, 95, 96
BURIAN, Emil, 96
BURNE-JONES, Sir Edward, 100
BURWELL PARISH CHURCH, Cam-
bridgeshire, 66
BUTLER, Henry Montague, 11
BUTT, Dame Clara, 47
BYAM SHAW ART COLLEGE, 138
BYRON, Lord, 46

CALVERT, Edward, 100, 145-46, 147,
159
CAMBRIDGE, 11, 12, 13, 14, 110, 115,
121, and passim
CAMBRIDGE AND COUNTY HIGH
SCHOOL FOR BOYS (now Sixth
Form College, Hills Road), 49-63 pas-
sim
CAMBRIDGE BOROUGH (now

CITY) CEMETERY, 57
CAMBRIDGE CREMATORIUM, 139
CAMBRIDGE DAILY NEWS, 111
CAMBRIDGE FORESTERS' BENEFIT
  BUILDING SOCIETY, 9
CAMBRIDGE MARKET, 30-33 *passim*,
  60
CAMBRIDGESHIRE SCHOOL OF
  ARTS, CRAFTS AND TECHNOL-
  OGY, 53
CAMBRIDGE UNIVERSITY MUSIC
  SOCIETY, 43
'CAM OBSERVATORY', 62
CAPERNAUM, 115
*CAPTAIN BRASSBOUND'S CONVER-
  SION* by George Bernard Shaw, 78
CARDUS, Neville, 44
CARELESS, George, 16
CARLYLE, Thomas, 45
CARMELITE CONVENTS, 67
CARNAVAL, Le, Ballet by Michel Fo-
  kine, music by Robert Schumann, 80
'CARROLL, LEWIS' (pseudonym of
  C.L. Dodgson), 44, 159
CARRYLL, Mary, 159
CARTER, Will, 79
CARTLEDGE, Horace Avron, 55
CART SHED AND LANE, Watercol-
  our by Samuel Palmer, 151
CASSE NOISETTE, Ballet by Lev Iva-
  nov, music by P.I. Tchaikovsky, 80
CASTLETON CHINA, 132
*CATALOGUE RAISONNÉ OF THE
  WORKS OF SAMUEL PALMER* by
  Raymond Lister, 148, 149, 150
CATHOLIC CHURCH OF OUR
  LADY AND THE ENGLISH MAR-
  TYRS, Cambridge, 25-26, 49
CATHOLIC PRIMARY SCHOOL,
  Cambridge, 26
CAVERSHAM, Suffolk, 156
CEYLON (now Sri Lanka), 42
CHAGALL, Marc, 107
CHALIAPIN, Feodor, 133
CHANCTONBURY RING, Sussex, 116
CHAPLIN, Charlie, 34, 48
'CHARITABLE GRINDERS', 39
CHARTERIS, Evan, 117
CHAUCER, Geoffrey, 109
CHEDDAR GORGE, 34
CHEDZOY, Alan, 154
CHEKHOV, Anton, 108
CHERRY ORCHARD by Anton Chek-
  hov, 108
CHESTERTON, G.K., 117

CHILDREN'S BIBLE Edited by Arthur
  Mee, 46
CHILDREN'S ENCYCLOPEDIA
  Edited by Arthur Mee, 45-46
CHILDREN'S NEWSPAPER Edited by
  Arthur Mee, 46
CHILDREN'S TREASURE HOUSE
  Edited by Arthur Mee, 46
CHOREUTICS, 88
CHRIST CHURCH, Cambridge, 36, 49
CHRISTMAS, 14-15, 18-19, 41, 92
CHRONICA, Ballet by Kurt Jooss,
  music by Berthold Goldschmidt, 86
CHURCH, *Canon* Edward Joseph, 49
CHURCHILL, *Sir* Winston S., 56
CINEMA, 41, 48-49, 52
CIRCUS, 12, 27, 34
CLARK, Eric, 59
CLAUDE OF LORRAINE, or
  CLAUDE GELLÉE, 105, 149, 156
CLAUDIUS, *Emperor* (Tiberius Clau-
  dius Nero Germanicus), 58
COBURG THEATRE, London, 155
COCKERELL, Sandy (Sydney M.),
  109, 138
COCKERELL, *Sir* Sydney Carlyle, 44,
  107
COCKERTONS, Linton, Cambridge-
  shire, 112, 119, 127
COCKINGTON, Devon, 91
COLLIER, John Payne, 30
COMMEDIA DELL' ARTE, 30
COMPANY AT THE MANOR, Ballet
  by Kurt Jooss, music by Beethoven,
  86
'CONSTRUMENTS', 61-62
COOK, *Professor* Arthur Bernard, 59
COOK, Olive, 136, 154
COPPÉLIA, Ballet by Lev Ivanov,
  music by Léo Delibes, 92, 93
CORVO, 'Baron' (Frederick Rolfe), 119
COSSA, Gabor, 134
COSWAY, Richard, 106
COUNTRY LIFE, 111
COURT, THE, Meldreth, Cambridge-
  shire, 130
COUSINS, Albert, 44-45, 59-60, 75,
  107, 109
COVENT GARDEN ROYAL OPERA,
  83, 94, 155
COVENT GARDEN RUSSIAN BAL-
  LET, 83
COVENTRY, 103
COWLEY, Abraham, 159
CRAIG, Edward Gordon, 77

CRASKE, Margaret, 91
CROXTON PARK, Cambridgeshire, 13
CRUCIFIXION by Tintoretto, 159
CUDWORTH, Charles, 89
CUMBERLAND, George, 120
CYMBELINE by William Shakespeare, 78
CYRIL COMES OVER by H.R. Tomalin, 78

DAILY MIRROR, 46
DAIROV, A., 135
DANCE NOTATION, 88-90
DANCING (other than ballet), 17-18, 19-20, 36-37, 92, 95-97, 99, 134-135
DANIELS, Bebe, 48-49
DANILOVA, Alexandra, 84
DARTINGTON HALL, Totnes, Devon, 85, 92, 95, 97
DARWIN, Charles, 141
DA SILVA PUPPET COMPANY, 138
DAVID, *King*, 6, 142
DAVID, Gustave, 60-61
DAVID, Hubert, 61, 77, 117, 121
DAVIDSON, Peter, 154
DA VINCI, Leonardo, 90
DE BEAUMONT, Comte Étienne, 83
DEGAS, Edgar, 133
DE LEMPICKA, Tamara, 106
DE MONTFORT, Lisa, 106, 124
DE MOSA, Noëlle, 86
DESIDERATA, Bibliographical periodical, 131
DE VALOIS, Ninette (Edris Stannus), 78, 80, 89, 94
DE ZOETE, Beryl, 92, 99
DIAGHILEV, Sergei Pavlovich, 80, 84, 85, 123, 132
DICKENS, Charles, 39, 51, 142, 157
DICKSON, Muriel, 77
DICTIONARY OF KINETOGRAPHY LABAN by Albrecht Knust, 134
DITAL HARP, 154
DODGSON, Charles Lutwidge. *See* Lewis Carroll.
DOGS, 7, 8, 21, 23, 111, 115, 147
DOLIN, Anton, 84, 137
DOLL'S HOUSE, A, by Henrik Ibsen, 80
DOMBEY AND SON, by Charles Dickens, 39
DONAT, Robert, 78
'DON BASILIO', 150
DONNE, John, 120
'DOONE VALLEY', Somerset, 93

'DOTHEBOYS HALL, GRETA BRIDGE', 51
D'OYLY CARTE OPERA COMPANY, 76-77
DRURY LANE THEATRE ROYAL, London, 83, 155

ECLOGUES of Virgil, 147
EDDINGTON, *Sir* Arthur, 140
EDE, Jim, 157
EDWARD VII, *King*, 58
EDWARDS, Mary Stella, 129
EGG, Augustus, 106
EGOROVA, Lyubov, 91
EGYPTOLOGY, 59, 77
EISENHOWER, *General* Dwight D. ('Ike'), 115
ELEVEN POEMS by Edmund Blunden, 129
ELIOT, T.S., 124
ELIZABETH I, *Queen*, 32
ELMHIRST, *Mr and Mrs* Leonard Knight, 92
ELOHIM, 143
EMBASSY BALLET, 94
ENDYMION by John Keats, 81
ENGINEERING, 5, 67-68, 155-156
ENGLEHEART, George, 106
ENTERTAINING, 153-155
ERNST, Max, 107
EROS, 109
ERTÉ (pseudonym of Romain de Tirtoff), 106
ESHKOL, Noa, 89
ESPINOSA, Judith, 91
ETON COLLEGE, 17, 32
ETTY, William, 105
EUAINETOS, 101
EUKINETICS, 88
EURHYTHMICS, 85
EXTER, Alexandra, 135
EYRE, Margery, 77

FABERGÉ, Carl, 100
FAIRHAVEN, *1st Lord*, 104-105
FAIRS, 14, 27-30, 34
FAKE'S PROGRESS by Tom Keating and others, 150
'FALSTAFF, Sir John', 132
FANCOURT, Darrell, 77
FANTIN-LATOUR, Henri, 59
FARLEIGH, John, 63
FARMING, 12, 13-14
FATHER AND SON by Edmund

Gosse, 112, 127
FAWCUS, Arnold, 147-148
FESTIVAL THEATRE, Cambridge, 77, 85
FESTIVAL THEATRE REVIEW, 123
FEUILLET, Raoul-Auger, 89
FEVER HOSPITAL, Cambridge, 38
FIDDLER OF DOONEY COMPETI-
TION, Sligo, 146
FIDELIO, opera by Beethoven, 142
FINCH, Francis Oliver, 145
FINCH, Rev. G.B., 65
FIREBIRD, THE. See Jar Ptitza
FITZWILLIAM MUSEUM, Cam-
bridge, 44-45, 59, 61, 75, 136
FLAMMARION, Camille, 61
FLATMAN, Thomas, 129
FLATTERS, Charles, 64
FLORENCE, 90
FLOWERS, 8, 31-32, 68, 157
FOKINE, Michel, 84
FOOD, 6, 14, 19, 23, 24, 110, 111
FORBES-ROBERTSON, Jean, 80
FORSTER, E.M., 32
FOX, Ernest William, 67-68
FRANCIS OF ASSISI, Saint, 73
FRANCIS, Thomas Musgrave, 13
FRIAR HOUSE RESTAURANT, Cam-
bridge, 88
FRINTON-ON-SEA, Essex, 140
FRITH, W.P., 106
FROGS of Aristophanes, 80, 125-126
FRY, C.B., 44, 125-126

GABHA by Raymond Lister, 128
GABO, Naum, 21
GAÎTÉ PARISIENNE, Ballet by Le-
onide Massine, music by Jacques Of-
fenbach, 83
GALLERIE DELL' ACCADEMIA,
Venice, 159
GAMES, 7, 33-34, 37
GAMLINGAY, Cambridgeshire, 11
GARDEN HOUSE HOTEL, Cam-
bridge, 131
GARDENS, 8, 31-32, 68, 104, 109
'GARGANTUA', 69
GARNETT, David, 85
GENESIS, 155
'GEORGE V' (steam engine), 28
GERTZ, Jenny, 96-98, 135
GIBBONS, Stanley, 21, 42
GIBBS, James, 75
GIFFORD, Gerald, 153-154
GILBERT, Sir William Schwenck, 47,
76
GILBEY, Monsignor Alfred Newman,
139
GIORGIONE (Giorgio Barbarelli), 149,
159
GISELLE; OU, LES WILIS, Ballet by
Théophile Gautier and Jean Coralli,
music by Adolphe Adam, 92
GOLDEN AGE, THE by Kenneth Gra-
hame, 159
GOLDEN COCKEREL PRESS, 123
GOLDEN HEAD PRESS, 123-137 pas-
sim, 154
GOOD SHEPHERD, THE, Unsigned
book for children, 22
GOSSE, Anna (Anna Gordon Keown),
111-112, 113-116, 119, 127, 130, 131,
139
GOSSE, Sir Edmund, 111-112, 117,
118, 127
GOSSE, Jennifer, 131
GOSSE, Philip, 111-112, 113-121, 124,
126, 130, 131, 139, 140
GOSSE, Philip Henry, 127
GOSSE, Sylvia, 118
GOULD, David, 150
GRAHAM, Martha, 86
GRAHAME, Helen, 159
GRAHAME, Kenneth, 159
GRAMMAR OF THE ART OF DANC-
ING by Friedrich Albert Zorn, 89
GRANVILLE, Sydney, 77
GRAY AND SON, John P., 79, 120
GRAY, Terence Stannus, 77-78, 79, 123
GREAT EXPECTATIONS by Charles
Dickens, 157
GREAT PYRAMID, 26
GREAT YARMOUTH, 12
GREENE, Graham, 40
GREEN TABLE, THE, Ballet by Kurt
Jooss, music by F.A. Cohen, 86
GRIEG, Edvard, 54, 95
GRIGGS, F.L., 159
GRIGSON, Geoffrey, 145
GRIMSHAW, Atkinson, 33
GROPIUS, Walter, 90
GUILDHALL, Cambridge, 31
GUINNESS, Arthur, 132
GUINNESS STOUT, 29, 146
GUTHRIE, Tyrone, 78

HADRIAN, Emperor (Publius Aelius
Hadrianus), 58
HAILEYBURY SCHOOL, Hertford-
shire, 49, 117

HALL, Anmer, 78
HALLS, Leonard, 43
*HANDBOOK OF KINETOGRAPHY
LABAN* by Albrecht Knust, 134
HANDEL, George Frederick, 20, 54
HARDY, Thomas, 61
HARROGATE, Yorkshire, 93
HARROW SCHOOL, 49, 56
HART, John, 93
HARVEY, F.E.E., 53-54
HARVEY, Frank, *junior*, 78-79
HARVEY, *Miss* J.M., 80
HARVEY, William, 120
HASSALL, Christopher, 103-104
HATTON, Harry, 56
HAWKE, *7th Lord, of Towton*, 5
HAWKING, Stephen, 141
HAWKS' CLUB, Cambridge, 39
HEADMASTERS' CONFERENCE, 49
HEDDA GABLER by Henrik Ibsen, 80
HEFFER, Emma Louise, 49
HEFFER, W., AND SONS LTD., 49, 63
HEFFER ART GALLERY, Cambridge,
97
HEGGENETT, Don Randle, 79
HENN, Thomas Rice, 129, 146
HENRY VI, *King*, 32
HENSHER, John, 97, 98-99
HIGGINS, Norman Openshaw, 80
HILLIARD, Nicholas, 106, 154
HISTORY OF BRITISH BIRDS by
Thomas Bewick, 40
HITLER, Adolf, 95
HOBBS, *Sir* Jack, 43
HOLBEIN, Hans, 100
HOLLAND, Vyvyan, 116
HOLLAR, Wenzel, 100
HOLLINGWORTH, Leonard ('Snap'),
55-56, 60, 63
HOLMES, Granny, 15-16
'HOLY JOE'. *See* Frederick Taylor.
HOLY TRINITY CHURCH, Cam-
bridge, 109
HOME GUARD, 115-116
HOMER, 131
HONER, Mary, 80, 90-94
HOOKHAM, John, 53
HOPPUS, E., 5
HOUGHTON HALL, Cambridge, 95,
96
HOUSEHOLD MANAGEMENT by Isa-
bella Beeton, 9
HOUSE OF LORDS, 112
HOWARD, Andrée, 85
HUMM, *Miss*, 36

HUTCHINSON, Ann, 89
HUXLEY, Alfred, 78-81 *passim*

IBSEN, Henrik, 80
ICOSAHEDRON, 88, 135
IDZIKOWSKI, Stanislas, 86
IF I WERE KING by Justin McCarthy,
79
IMPERIAL SCHOOL OF BALLET, St
Petersburg, 84
INDIA, 99, 100
INEDITED WORKS OF BAKST by
Valerian Svetlov *and others*, 133
INGOLDSBY LEGENDS by R.H. Bar-
ham, 40
I SEE ALL Edited by Arthur Mee, 46
ISLE OF MAN, 87
ISOLA BELLA, 115
ISRAEL, 89
ITCH, *Miss*, 110
IVANOV, Lev, 84

'JACKDAW, THE'. *See Sir* Geoffrey
Keynes
JAMES, *Rev.* C.C.H., 73
JANNINGS, Emil, 48
JAPAN, 129
JARMAN, W.R., 57, 63
JAR PTITZA (The Firebird), 124
JERUSALEM, Poem by William Blake,
142
JESUS, 22, 23, 27, 115
JESUS COLLEGE, Cambridge, 31
JONES, David, 107
JOOSS, Aino. *See* Aino Siimola
JOOSS, Kurt, 87-88, 95, 97, 99, 135
JOOSS-LEEDER SCHOOL OF
DANCE, 97
JUNGLE BOOKS by Rudyard Kipling,
44

KEATING, Tom, 150-152
KEATON, Buster, 48
KEATS, John, 81, 120, 159
KELMSCOTT PRESS, 59
KEMP, Travis, 94
KEOWN, Anna Gordon. *See* Anna
Gosse
KEOWN, Eric, 112
KETTLE'S YARD, Cambridge, 157
KEYNES, *Sir* Geoffrey, 79, 103-104,
119-122, 130, 139, 145, 147, 148
KEYNES, John Maynard, *Lord*, 80, 121-

122, 139
KEYNES, *Lady* [Margaret], (née Darwin; wife of Sir Geoffrey Keynes), 119, 120, 139
KIEV, 133
KILVERT, Francis, 156
KIMON, 100
KINETOGRAPHY LABAN, 88-90, 133-134
KING, Jack, 121, 149
KING LEAR by William Shakespeare, 142
KING'S COLLEGE, Cambridge, 32, 67, 71, 75, 121, 139
KINGSFORD, Florence (wife of *Sir* Sydney Cockerell), 106-07
KING'S LYNN, 30
KIPLING, Rudyard, 44, 117
KNUST, Albrecht, 133-134
KRÖLLER, Heinrich, 95
KUZNETSOVA, Maria, 124

LABAN, Rudolf von, 85, 87-90 *passim*, 96, 97, 99, 135
LABANOTATION. *See* Kinetography Laban
LAC DES CYGNES, LE, Ballet by Marius Petipa and Lev Ivanov, music by P.I. Tchaikovsky, 84, 137
LADY INTO FOX, Ballet by Andrée Howard, music by Arthur Honegger, 85
LAKE, Molly, 94
LAMB, B. J. *See* 'Uncle Dick'
LANDSEER, *Sir* Edwin, 105
LANG, Fritz, 52
LANT, Humphrey, 19-20, 47, 62
LAOCOÖN, 144
LAPAGE, Geoffrey, 127
LAURENCIN, Marie, 106
LAYNG, T.P.R., 55
LEAMINGTON, 61
'LEAR, King', 142
LEE, S. *and* S., 61
LEEDER, Sigurd, 87-89 *passim*, 134, 135
LEGAT, Nicolas, 91
LEIGHTON, Frederick, *Lord*, 106
LENINGRAD, 124, 132
LENOX CHINA, 132
LEVINSON, André, 133
LEWIN, James Arthur, 30
LEWIS, Bertha, 77
LIFE AND LETTERS OF SIR EDMUND GOSSE by Evan Charteris, 117

LIGHT, Edward, 154
'LIGHTNING' (Siggers), 31
LING, Arthur, 103
LINNELL *FAMILY,* 149
LINNELL, John, 100, 149
LINTON, Cambridgeshire, 112, 153-154
LISSIM, Dorothea (wife of Simon Lissim), 132, 139
LISSIM, Simon, 124, 133, 136, 139
LISTER, Alfred, 5, 9, 19, 64, 65
LISTER, Alice ('Bet'), 8, 19
LISTER, Ambrose, 1
LISTER, Arthur, 5
LISTER, Brian Horace, 65, 126
LISTER, Delia, 40, 138-139
LISTER (née Arnold; my mother), Ellen Maud Mary, 1, 11, 19, 21, 23-25, 27, 47, 57, 71, 74, 109
LISTER, Emily Maude, 8, 19
LISTER, Fanny, 5, 6-8
LISTER, Frances Emily (my grandmother), 5, 6-10 *passim*, 18
LISTER, Frederick, 5
LISTER, George (my grandfather), 5-10 *passim*, 18, 26, 46, 61, 62, 64, 67, 69, 70
LISTER, George (my great grandfather), 1, 5
LISTER, George, *and Sons Ltd.*, 21, 28, 64-72 *passim*, 102, 105 *passim*
LISTER, Harry, 5, 6
LISTER, Horace (my father), 1, 5, 18, 19, 21, 23, 26-27, 45-46, 56-57, 60, 64, 69-72, 77-78, 103, 109, 126
LISTER, Josiah, 1
LISTER, Pamela Helen (my wife), 40, 108-111 *passim*, 116, 118, 119, 120, 124, 129, 137, 138, 139, 140, 146, 147, 154-160 *passim*
LISTER, Raymond George. *Ancestry*, 1-5, 11, 13; *Birth*, 1; *Childhood*, 1-63 *passim; Family gatherings and parties*, 18-20; *Schools: St. Clair School (Miss Royston's)*, 36-39; *St. John's College Choir School*, 39-45 *passim; Cambridge and County High School for Boys*, 49-63 *passim; Puberty*, 50, 51-52; *Illnesses*, 37-38, 49; *Neuroses and fears*, 27, 56-57, 139-140; *Religious struggles and beliefs*, 25-27, 57, 72-74, 139-144; *Apprenticeship*, 64-70; *Blacksmithery*, 64-67, 102-105 *passim*, 128, 155-156; *Books and publishing*, 99, 123-137, 145-146, 148-150; *Cinema*, 48-49; *Mini-*

ature painting and other forms of visual art, 43, 53, 59-60, 76, 81-82, 99-101, 105-107, 123, 124, 126, 127-128, 136-137; *Theatre*, 7, 16, 17, 24, 34, 76-81, 83-99 *passim*, 108, 124, 132-135 *passim*, 153-155, 158; *Romance* , 48-49, 77, 81-82, 90-94, 101, 108-109, 153-154; *Marriage*, 108-110
LISTER, Rory, 40, 131, 138, 139
LISTER, William, 1, 9
LITTLE THEATRE AT WINDMILL HOUSE, Linton, Cambridgeshire, 153-155
LLANGOLLEN, Ladies of (Sarah Ponsonby and Lady Eleanor Butler), 159
LLOYD, Harold, 48
LLOYD JONES, *Dr*. Ernest, 45, 57, 71, 72
LOBB, William, 157
LODGE, *Sir* Oliver, 26, 141
LONDON, CITY OF, 67, 102
LONDON ZOO, 22, 23
LONG MELFORD, Suffolk, 129
LOPOKOVA, Lydia (*Lady* Keynes), 80, 84, 121
LORNA DOONE bv ℞ ꭰ Blackmore, 93
LOUKOMSKI, Georgi, 132
LOW COUNTRIES, 41, 59, 91
LOWEY, W.J., 51
LOW THATCH, West Wratting, Cambridgeshire, 109-111 *passim*
LU CHI, 100
LYCEUM THEATRE, London, 155
LYONS, H. Agar, 48
LYTTON, *Sir* Henry, 77

MACBETH by William Shakespeare, 40
McCARTHY, Justin, 79
McCORMICK, Joseph Coneybeare, 43
McCOR MICK, *Rev*. 'Pat', 43
MACDONALD AND EVANS *Ltd*., 134
MACHINERY, 64-65, 67-68, 69, 155-156
MACLEOD, Joseph Gordon, 78
MAGDALENE COLLEGE, Cmbridge, 5
MAGRITTE, René, 107
MAHLER, Gustav, 20
MALINS, Edward, 129
MANCHESTER, 93
MANN WORDIE, *Sir* James *and Lady*, 103
MANTELL, Gilbert, 54-55

MANUFACTURE NATIONALE DE SÈVRES, 132
MARC, Franz, 107
MARINA, *Duchess of Kent*, 105
MARKET HILL, Cambridge, 30-33 *passim*
MARSHALL, Norman, 78
MARTIN, John, 6
MARY, *Blessed Virgin*, 23, 59
MARY, *Queen*, 48
MASK THEATRE, London, 99
MASON, Samuel Albert, 66-67
MASSINE, Leonide, 83-84, 89
MASSINE ON CHOREOGRAPHY by Leonide Massine, 89
MAUGHAM, William Somerset, 77
MAY (housemaid of *Rev*. and *Mrs*. S. Senior), 40
MAYFIELD, John S., 121
MAYNE, Arthur Brinley ('Tishy'), 49-63 *passim*
MEE, Arthur, 45-46
MELBOURNE HALL, Derbyshire, 103
MELDRETH, Cambridgeshire, 130
MEMOIRS OF A FOX-HUNTING MAN by Siegfried Sassoon, 130, 131
MEMORIES AND PORTRAITS by Robert Louis Stevenson, 117
MENON, Narayana, 99
MERCHANT OF VENICE, THE by William Shakespeare, 40
MICHELANGELO BUONARROTI, 100, 142
MIDSUMMER COMMON, Cambridge, 14, 27-30 *passim*
MILLS, Bertram, 27
MILTON, John, 46, 147, 149
MINIATURE PAINTING AND MINIATURE ARTS, 23, 44, 59-60, 81, 99-101, 105-107, 109, 125, 127, 154
MIR ISKUSSTVA (The World of Art), 133
MISSEN, Harold, 34-35
MODERN DANCE, 83-99 *passim*
MOORE, Thomas Sturge, 159
MORLEY, Robert, 78
MORRIS, Cynthia M., 136
MORRIS, William, 59, 106
MOSCOW, 124
MOSES, 148
MOTOR CARS, 34
MOUNT NEBO, 148
MOZART, Wolfgang Amadeus, 20
MUIR, Percy, 118-119
MUNICH STATE OPERA, 95

MUNNINGS, *Sir* Alfred, 105
MURPHY, Frank, 75
MUSCOVITE PEACOCK, THE, by
Raymond Lister, 124, 127, 132
MUSIC, 19-20, 23, 24, 28, 32, 47-48, 54,
58, 146, 153-154
MY MAGAZINE Edited by Arthur
Mee, 46

NAZIS, 88
NEWMAN, *Cardinal* John Henry, 8
NEWMARKET, Suffolk, 14, 110
NEWMARKET ROAD GOSPEL
MISSION, Cambridge, 11
NEWNHAM, Cambridge, 129
NEW THEATRE, Cambridge, 76-77
NEWTON, *Sir* Douglas *and Lady* (later
Lord and Lady Eltisley), 13
NICHOLSON, *Sir* William, 61
NIJINSKA, Bronislava, 84
NIJINSKY, Vaslav Fomich, 85
NIKE, 59
'NODDY'. *See* Harry Brown
NONESUCH PRESS, 123
NORMAN, Geraldine, 150
NOVERRE, Jean-Georges, 134
NOYE'S FLUDDE by Don Randle
Heggenett, 79
NUGENT, Mollie (stage-name of Max
Arnold, *q.v.*), 17
NUMISMATICS, 58-59
NUTCRACKER, Ballet by Lev Ivanov,
music by P.I. Tchaikovsky, 80
NYREN, John, 128

'OAKEY', 31
'ODETTE', 84, 92
OFFENBACH, Jacques, 83
OLD SHIP HOTEL, Brighton, 91
*ONE THOUSAND BEAUTIFUL
THINGS* Edited by Arthur Mee, 46
OPEN AIR THEATRE, Regent's Park,
London, 94
OSBORNE, Malcolm, 76
O.T.C. AT COUNTY SCHOOL, Cam-
bridge, 54-55
OTHELLO by William Shakespeare, 40
OXFORD, 62, 79, 125, 145
OXFORD UNIVERSITY PRESS, 149

PALMER, Samuel, 46, 100, 145, 148-
151, 156, 157, 159
PAMELA'S PLEASURE and *RAY-*

MOND'S RELISH by Gerald Gif-
ford, 153-154
PARFITT, P.A., 123
PARIS, 124, 132, 133, 135, 147
PARKER, Clifton, 97
PARKER, 'Sluice', 31-32
PARKER'S PIECE, Cambridge, 33
PARSONS, David, 154
PARTHENON, 101
PARTY POLITICS, 12-13
PASK, Robert ('Bobby'), 51-52, 55
PASTON HOUSE. *See* St. Mary's Con-
vent School, Cambridge
*PASTORAL WITH A HORSE-CHEST-
NUT,* Watercolour by Samuel Pal-
mer, 151
PATMORE, Coventry, 117
PATMORE, Epiphany ('Piffy'), 117
PAUL, *Tsar*, 48
PAVLOVA, Anna, 133
PAYNE, Austin B., 46
PEARSON, *Mrs*, 126
PEARSON, Arthur, 16
PECK, G., *and Son Ltd.*, 45
'PELLÉAS AND MÉLISANDE', 82
PEMBROKE COLLEGE, Cambridge,
75, 114
PEPYS, Samuel, 124
PERSIA (now Iran), 100
PETIPA, Marius, 84
PETRARCH (Francesco Petrarca), 157
PEVSNER, *Sir* Nikolaus, 103
PHENOMENON OF MAN, THE by
Pierre Teilhard de Chardin, 141
PHILATELY, 21-22, 23, 54
PHILIP, George, *and Son Ltd.*, 61
'PHRYNE', 124
PILGRIM'S PROGRESS, THE by John
Bunyan, 41
'PIP, SQUEAK AND WILFRED', 46-47
PLAYBOX, Weekly for children, 37
POE, Edgar Allan, 56
POISONED KISS, THE, comic opera
by Ralph Vaughan Williams, 80
'POPSKI', 46-47
POPULAR ASTRONOMY by Camille
Flammarion, 61
PORLOCK, Somerset, 93-94
POWELL, William, 48
POWERS, Alan, 154
POYNTER, Ambrose, 36
POYNTZ, Newdigate ('Two, four, six,
eight'), 58
PRACTICAL MEASURER by E.
Hoppus, 5

PRAGUE, 96
PRATT, MANNING, tailors, Cambridge, 104
PREOBRAZHENSKAYA, Olga, 84
PRIOR, Camille, 87
PRIVATE LIBRARIES ASSOCIATION, 136
PROCTOR, Ernest, 116
PROMISED LAND, 148
PUNCH, Weekly magazine, 112
PUNCH AND JUDY SHOW, 7,30-31, 34
PURCELL, Henry, 54

QUEEN MARY HALL, Great Russell Street, London, 134
QUEST FOR CORVO, THE, by A.J.A. Symons, 119
QUY, Cambridgeshire, 13

RADIO, 21-22, 35, 99
RADIO-LOCATION, 85
RADIUM INSTITUTE, London, 118
RAIN by W. Somerset Maugham, 77
RAINBOW, Weekly for children, 37
RAKE'S PROGRESS, THE, Ballet by Ninette de Valois, music by Gavin Gordon, 80
RAMBERT, Dame Marie, 85-87
RAMPANT LIONS PRESS, 79
RANDS, Leslie, 77
'RANEVSKY, Madam and Anya', 108
RASH, Billy, 110, 111
RATTEE AND KETT, Ltd., builders, Cambridge, 32
RATTRAY, Rev.R.F., 140
RAVERAT, Gwendolen, 80
RAWLINGS, Margaret, 78
RAYMOND by Sir Oliver Lodge, 26
READING UNIVERSITY LIBRARY, 136
RECUEIL DE DANSES by Raoul Auger Feuillet, 89
REINHART, Max, 98
RELIGION, 5-6, 11, 18, 25-27, 49, 72-74, 109, 140-144
REMBRANDT HARMENSZOON VAN RIJN, 149
REPTON SCHOOL, Derby, 124
REYNOLDS, Graham, 147
REYNOLDS FAMILY, Confectioners, Cambridge, 34
RIABOUCHINSKA, Tatiana, 84
RICHMOND, George, 46, 100, 145

RICKETTS, Charles, 100
RIDGE, Harold, 77
RIVIÈRE AND SON, 121
ROBERTS, Mr. (The Gosses' plumber), 114
ROBERTS, David, 103
ROBERTS, Sir S.C., 114-115
ROBINSON, Sir David, 56
ROBINSON, Henry Crabb, 128
ROBSON, Flora, 78
RODGERS AND HAMMERSTEIN, 47
RODNEY DRAMATIC CLUB, Cambridge, 79
ROLFE, Victor, 118
'ROMEO AND JULIET', 82
ROOPE, Joe, 110-111
ROOPE, Sid, 110
ROOTHAM, Dr Cyril B., 43, 80
ROOTHAM, Helen, 43
ROSE, Clarkson, 115
ROSE, George, 30
ROSENWALD, Lessing J., 148
ROSNER, Arpad, 96
ROSSETTI, Dante Gabriel, 23
ROSSINI, Giacomo, 20
ROSSITER'S ART SHOP, Cambridge, 79
ROTTERDAM, 91
ROUND CHURCH HALL, Cambridge, 75-76
ROUSE, Bill, 68
ROWE, Mr., 104
ROYAL AUTOMOBILE CLUB, 126
ROYAL BALLET, 80
ROYAL HORTICULTURAL SOCIETY, 127
ROYAL HOTEL, Cambridge, 131
ROYAL SOCIETY OF MINIATURE PAINTERS, SCULPTORS AND GRAVERS, 105-106
ROYSTON, Emma, 36-37
RUBINSTEIN, Ida, 133
RUGBY SCHOOL, Warwickshire, 49
RUISDAEL, Jakob van, 149
RYDER, William, 59
RYLANDS, George ('Dadie'), 80

'SABRA, Princess', 95
SAFFRON WALDEN, Essex, 110
SAILOR'S FANCY, Ballet by Sigurd Leeder, music by Martin Penny, 86
ST. ALBAN'S SCHOOL, Cambridge, 95
ST. ANDREW'S STREET BAPTIST CHAPEL, Cambridge, 5

ST. CATHARINE'S COLLEGE, Cambridge, 79
ST. CLAIR SCHOOL, Cambridge, 36-39 *passim*
ST. DOMINIC'S PRESS, 123
SAINT GEORGE by Raymond Lister, 95
ST. GILES'S CHURCH, Cambridge, 73
ST. JOHN'S COLLEGE, Cambridge, 43, 103
ST. JOHN'S COLLEGE CHOIR SCHOOL, Cambridge, 39-45 *passim*, 49, 60
ST. MARTIN-IN-THE-FIELDS CHURCH, London, 43
ST. MARY'S CONVENT SCHOOL (Paston House), Cambridge, 16, 17, 36
ST. PETER'S, Rome, 100
ST. PETERSBURG, 124, 132
ST. SEBASTIANO'S, Venice, 159
SALZBURG, 98
SAMUEL PALMER: A VISION RECAPTURED by Arnold Fawcus, Sir Geoffrey Keynes, Raymond Lister and Graham Reynolds, 147
SAMUEL PALMER'S ITALIAN HONEYMOON by Edward Malins, 129
SANGER, *'Lord'* George, 27
SAPPHO, 121
SASBURG, Yoma, 97
SASSOON, Siegfried, 119, 128, 130-132
SCHLEMMER, Oskar, 90
SCHOOL VIRGIL (The Pastorals of Virgil, with a Course of English Reading adapted for Schools...by Robert John Thornton), 148
SCUOLA GRANDE DI SAN ROCCO, Venice, 159
SEARLE, Ronald, 53
'SELINA', 159
SELWYN COLLEGE, Cambridge, 67
SENATE HOUSE, Cambridge, 75
SENIOR, Mariam (wife of Rev. S. Senior), 43
SENIOR, *Rev.* Sam, 40-42, 73-74, 109
SEVEN HEROES, THE, Ballet by Kurt Jooss, music by Henry Purcell, 86
SHADRACH, MESHACH AND ABEDNEGO, 6
SHAKESPEARE, William, 40, 46, 78, 80, 94, 124, 130, 132, 142
'SHALLOW, Justice', 132
SHAW, George Bernard, 63, 78, 117

SHERLOCK, Marjorie, 76, 97
SHERMAN, Welby, 145
SHERSTON'S PROGRESS, by Siegfried Sassoon, 131
SHIPP, *Miss*, 16
SHOREHAM, Kent, 151, 159
SHOREHAM AT TWILIGHT, pastiche by Tom Keating, 151
SHRUBBS, Harold, 59
SICKERT, Walter Richard, 76, 118
SIDDALL, Lizzie, 124
SIIMOLA, Aino (*Mrs* Kurt Jooss), 87
'SIN FANG, Dr', 48
SINGAPORE, 58
SISTINE CHAPEL, Vatican City, 100, 142
SITWELL *FAMILY*, 159
SITWELL, *Dame* Edith, 43
SITWELL, *Sir* Sacheverell, 127, 130
SLADE SCHOOL OF ART, 156
SLIGO, 145-147
SMITH, Edwin, 136, 154
SMITH, *Canon* Sydney, 143
SMYTH, *Rev.* Charles, 73
'SNAP'. *See* Leonard Hollingworth
SOCIETY FOR PSYCHICAL RESEARCH, 141
SOLAR PHYSICS OBSERVATORY, Cambridge, 61-62
SONGS, 12, 19
SONGS OF INNOCENCE by William Blake, 44, 128
SONGS OF INNOCENCE AND EXPERIENCE by William Blake, 128
SORENSEN, Carl, and Son, Copenhagen, 132
SORT OF LIFE, A, by Graham Greene, 40
SPAIN, 41
SPEAIGHT, George, 154-155
SPENSER, Edmund, 159
SPORT, 43-44, 129
SPRING TALE, A, Ballet by Kurt Jooss, music by F.A. Cohen, 86
'SQUEERS, Wackford', 51
SQUIRE, *Sir* J.C., 116
STAGEMAN, Peter, 127
STALIN, Josef, 97
STANNUS, Edris. *See* Ninette de Valois
STAR BREWERY, Cambridge, 36, 68-69
STATION HOTEL, Cambridge, 18
STEPANOV, V.I., 89
STETCHWORTH DAIRIES, Cam-

bridge, 75
STEVENSON, Robert Louis, 117, 119
STEWART, Meum, 124
STONE, Reynolds, 103
STONEBRIDGE, Blanche, 36-37
STRAVINSKY, Igor, 20
STRESA, 115
STURT, George, 1.
'SUGAR PLUM FAIRY', 80, 92
SULLIVAN, *Sir* Arthur, 47, 76
SUNBEAM, Weekly for Children, 37
SUNDAY TIMES, 112
SURREY THEATRE, London, 155
SUTHERLAND, Graham, 75
SVETLOV, Valerian, 133
'SWANILDA', 91-92, 93
SWANSEA, 49
SWINBURNE, Algernon Charles, 121
SWITZERLAND, 115
'SYLPHIDE, LA', 87
SYMONS, A.J.A., 116, 118-119
SYRACUSE, 59

TAGLIONI, Marie, 88
TANNER, Robin *and* Heather, 156, 159
TANZARCHIV, DAS, Hamburg, 134
TATHAM, Frederick *and* Arthur, 145
TAYLOR, Frederick ('Holy Joe'), 52, 56
TCHAIKOVSKY, Peter Ilyich, 20
'TEBRICK, Mrs.', 85
TEILHARD DE CHARDIN, Pierre, 141
TELEVISION, 35
*TEMPEST*A by Giorgione, 159
TENNYSON, Alfred, *Lord*, 46, 141, 159
THEATRE ROYAL, BARNWELL (*see* Festival Theatre), 77
THEBES, 100
THERE WAS A STAR DANCED... by Raymond Lister, 137
THOMAS, Dylan, 154
THOMPSON, Leonard W. ('Tommy'), 79
THORNTON, Robert John, 148
'THREE GRACES OF CAMBRIDGE', 31-32
THROUGH THE LOOKING GLASS AND WHAT ALICE FOUND THERE by Lewis Carroll (C.L. Dodgson), 159
TIGER TIM'S WEEKLY, Weekly for Children, 37
TIMES, THE, 150
TIMES LITERARY SUPPLEMENT, THE, 127
TINTORETTO (Jacopo Robusti), 159

'TINY TIM', 29
'TISHY'. *See* Arthur Brinley Mayne
TITIAN (Tiziano Vecelli), 149
TITLE TO PHOEBE, A, by Raymond Lister, 137
TITLE LIST OF BOOKS ON MINIATURE PAINTING, A, by Raymond Lister, 123
TOKYO, 129
TOLFORD MANOR, near Canterbury, 103
TOLSTOY, Lev, 131, 142
TOMALIN, H.R., 78
TOMLINSON, Kellom, 89
TOM SAWYER by Mark Twain (Samuel Langhorne Clemens), 44
TOTNES, Devon, 92
TOUMANOVA, Tamara, 84
TOY THEATRE PLAYS
(*The Battle of Waterloo; The Sleeping Beauty in the Wood; The Corsican Brothers, or, The Fatal Duel*), 154
TRAVERS, Ben, 79
TREASURE ISLAND by Robert Louis Stevenson, 120
TREATISE CONCERNING THE ARTE OF LIMNING by Nicholas Hilliard, 106
TREATISE OF PROBABILITY by John Maynard Keynes, 122
TRIADIC BALLET by Oskar Schlemmer, music by Paul Hindemith, 90
TRIANON PRESS, Paris, 147-148
TRINITY COLLEGE, Cambridge, 32, 115
'TRISTAN AND ISOLDE', 82
TUBALCAIN, 155
TUGAL, Pierre, 124
TURKEY, 100
TURNER, Harold, 91
TWAIN, MARK (Samuel Langhorne Clemens), 44
'TWANKEY, Widow', 115
'TWO, FOUR, SIX, EIGHT'. *See* Newdigate Poyntz

ULLMANN, Lisa, 134, 135
'UNCLE DICK' (B.J. LAMB), 46
UNIVERSITY OF ARTS SOCIETY, Cambridge, 75-76
UNIVERSITY BALLET CLUB, Cambridge, 87
UPPINGHAM SCHOOL, Leicestershire, 49
'URIZEN' 49

VALLEY OF VISION, THE, SEPHAM BARN, SHOREHAM, Watercolour by Samuel Palmer, 150
VANNI, Andrea, 59
VAUGHAN WILLIAMS, Ralph, 80
VENICE, 159
VERDI, Giuseppe, 20
VERONESE, Paul (Paolo Caliari), 159
VESPASIAN, *Emperor* (Titus Flavius Vespasianus), 58
VICTORIA AND ALBERT MUSEUM, 147, 151
VIC-WELLS BALLET, 16, 80, 84, 90-94 *passim*
VILLA D'ESTE, Tivoli, 28
VIRGIL (Publius Vergilius Maro), 147, 148, 149

WACHMANN, Abraham, 89
WADDESDON, Buckinghamshire, 103
WALEY, Arthur, 92
WALKER, Nea, 26
WALLACE, Edgar, 9
WALLACE, Lew, 41
WALLS, Tom, 79
WALTER, Henry, 145
WARNER, Francis, 129, 145, 149
WAUGH, Arthur, 116
WAUGH, Evelyn, 117
WAY by Laurence Whistler, 128
WEBB, Joseph, 159
WEBBER-DOUGLAS ACADEMY OF DRAMATIC ART, 138
WEBSTER, Clive, 154
WEBSTER, Eva, 25-26
WEDDING BOUQUET, A, Ballet by Frederick Ashton, music by Lord Berners, 92, 94
WELLINGTON, *Duke of,* 159
'WEMMICK, John', 157
WEPPONS, Sussex, 116, 119
'WERTHER, YOUNG', 82
WESTROP, T., 72
WEST WRATTING, Cambridgeshire, 109-111 *passim,* 119, 120
WHADDON, Cambridgeshire, 58
WHEELWRIGHT'S SHOP, THE, by

George Sturt, 1
WHISTLER, Laurence, 128, 156
WHISTLER, Rex, 106
WHITAKER, F.R., 58-59
WHITAKER'S *ALMANACK,* 9
WHO'S WHO, 131
WHO'S WHO IN HEAVEN by Clifford Bax, 124-125
WIGMAN, Mary, 99
WILFREDIAN LEAGUE OF GUG-NUNCS, 47
WILLIAM IV, *King,* 5
WILLIAM BLAKE TRUST, 147-148
WILSON, *Mr.,* 44
WIND IN THE WILLOWS, THE by Kenneth Grahame, 159
WINDMILL HOUSE, Linton, Cambridgeshire, 153-154
WINDSOR CASTLE, 105
WODEHOUSE, P.G., 71, 126
WOLFSON COLLEGE, Cambridge, 121, 149
WORLD OF ART. See *Mir Iskusstva*
WOMEN'S INSTITUTE, 111
WORLD WAR I, 1, 9, 31, 55, 65, 117, 120
WORLD WAR II, 13, 35, 58, 85, 86, 88, 91, 102, 123, 124, 129, 148
WORSHIPFUL COMPANY OF BLACKSMITHS, 102
WREN, *Sir* Christopher, 75
'WTZKOFFSKI', 47

YALE CENTER FOR BRITISH ART, 150
YEATS, Gráinne, 146
YEATS, Michael, 146
YEATS, W.B., 145-147
YOUNG CRICKETER'S TUTOR by John Nyren, 128
YOUNGHUSBAND, *Miss,* 110

ZORN, Friedrich Albert, 89
ZÜLLIG, Hans, 86